Motorcycle

Objekt

Titles in the *Objekt* series explore a range of types – buildings, products, artefacts – that have captured the imagination of modernist designers, makers and theorists. The objects selected for the series are by no means all modern inventions, but they have in common the fact that they acquired a particular significance in the last 100 years.

In the same series

Factory
Gillian Darley

Aircraft
David Pascoe

Motorcycle

Steven E. Alford and Suzanne Ferriss

REAKTION BOOKS

For Gary Kieffner

Published by Reaktion Books Ltd
33 Great Sutton Street
London EC1V 0DX, UK
www.reaktionbooks.co.uk

First published 2007

Printed and bound in China

British Library Cataloguing in Publication Data
Alford, Steven E., 1950–
    Motorcycle. – (Objekt)
    1. Motorcycles – History   2. Motorcycling – Social aspects
    3. Motorcycling – History
    I. Title II. Ferriss, Suzanne, 1962–
    629.2'275'09

    ISBN–13: 978 1 86189 345 1
    ISBN–10: 1 86189 345 0

Contents

Introduction

James Boswell, although a man of many words, doesn't report on the donkey's perspective on hauling the bulk of Samuel Johnson around the Hebrides. We do know, however, what Dr Johnson himself thought of travel and the pleasures of speed. 'If . . . I had no duties, and no reference to futurity, I would spend my life in driving briskly in a post-chaise with a pretty woman; but she should be one who could understand me, and would add something to the conversation.'[1] One naturally wonders about his attitude toward placing her on the pillion seat of a motorcycle – he would no doubt require wireless headsets to communicate his observations.

It seems simple enough: strap a motor to a bicycle, transfer the engine's rotational energy to one of the wheels, and you have a motorcycle. Yet, to anyone who has seen Valentino Rossi scrape a puck down to nothing through a chicane or read of Dr Gregory Frazier conquering yet another continent, contemporary motorcycles are anything but simple machines. Purpose-driven design has produced devices of power and beauty unparalleled in the world of transportation. From the Indonesian fisherman's scooter that brings his catch to market to the 2000cc cruiser that carries a couple from Miami to Yellowknife, a motorcycle's form so exquisitely

Power meets beauty.

follows its function that Melissa Holbrook Pierson rightly called it 'The Perfect Vehicle'.[2]

While practical function properly determines the motorcycle's form, its function doesn't exist in isolation. As a design object, we can say that the motorcycle has three functions: its practical function, to move a person about; an aesthetic function, to please the senses; and a symbolic function, to transmit social information about the rider and who he or she is.[3] Hence the motorcycle is infused with cultural significance, tied up with complex issues of history, technology, engineering, consumerism, psychology, aesthetics, gender and sexuality. In that respect, the motorcycle is a nexus of social and cultural relations, an instrument of identity formation for the rider, a pop culture icon, and an aesthetic object in its own right. While the motorcycle owner is most often featured culturally as an icon of rebellion, the motorcycle can represent patriotic nationalism, in the figure of the German *Kradschützen* (motorcycle infantry); gendered independence, as women from Theresa Wallach to Katja Poensgen have demonstrated; middle-class 'niceness', as Soichiro Honda's 1963 press agents would have it; or stand as an ambiguous figure of state power, as we see in the film *Electra Glide in Blue* (1973).

Whatever the contemporary image of the motorcyclist, it doesn't match the reality. In the US, for example, the average motorcycle owner in 2003 was 41 years old, with a median household income of $55,850. 29 per cent had college degrees.[4] (By contrast, in 1980 the typical owner was 24 years old and earned $17,500.)[5] Or consider the role of the motorcycle in developing countries: hardly a symbol of rebellion, the motorcycle is an essential element in the economies of countries populated by small-time, independent entrepreneurs, from bakers to souvenir vendors. While the contemporary motorcycle is designed to achieve cutting edge results, whether the goal is speed, distance or endurance, worldwide the motorcycle is most often employed by a proletarian worker or a 'weekend warrior', whose principal use of the machine is to haul him around on a Saturday afternoon. As with the racing car, the capacities of contemporary motorcycles on display on the racetrack are primarily a showcase for the capitalist business of moving as many units as possible from the showroom into private hands.

In this book, we approach the motorcycle as a design object by examining four areas. In Chapter 1 we survey key developments in the history of motorcycle design, considering the transition from bicycle to motorcycle, technical improvements to early internal combustion engines and the challenges of producing motorcycles for sale. We emphasize the purpose-driven designs of motorcycles, as well as design considerations external to the bike itself. Next, in Chapter 2, we explore the fascinating connections between the motorcycle and identity formation, looking at the Japanese *bosozoku* phenomenon, the heyday of the British Mods and Rockers, the workings of the American motorcycle clubs and the changing attitudes toward women and motorcycling. In Chapter 3, we examine popular images of the bike and its riders, not simply the leather-clad, proletarian thug first popularized in the 1950s, but other images proffered in song, literature and the movies, from the boy's book *Tom Swift and his Motorcycle* to Marianne Faithfull's erotic portrayal of a 'girl' on a motorcycle to *The World's Fastest Indian*. Finally, in Chapter 4, we consider the bike shorn of its rider, as an aesthetic object worthy (or unworthy) of contemplation, and its role in displaying rider style. While various Guggenheim shows have popularized the bike's appearance, we discuss other ways in which the bike has been considered as Art, from the Italian Futurists to motorcycle designers.

Motorcycles are dangerous, thrilling, loud, environmentally sensitive, sexy, threatening, lucrative, a hole where your money goes,

Female Buddhist monks ride a motorcycle, Ho Chi Minh City, Vietnam, 2005.

good for women, irresistible to those with a death wish, seductive, off-putting, a reliable transportation device, a mass of chrome with oil leaking from the bottom, your best friend, something to annoy the neighbours with, an expression of your freedom as a citizen, a transgression of your rights as an insurance risk, the perfect vehicle, a Japanese threat to Western economies, the ideal marriage of technology and aesthetics, a test of the limits of human driving competence, a toy for boys, a machine of war, a means of travel that promotes human harmony, transportation only good for ignorant proles, a device for dentists to play the outlaw on weekends, something to buy and modify to make it your own, a rich person's purchased 'individuality', an outmoded transportation device hindering the development of 'intelligent transportation systems', a means to

The October 2005 'Biketoberfest' motorcycle festival held in Daytona Beach, Florida.

beat the high price of petrol, a device for bringing the family together, something to do with the boys where the wife isn't allowed, a design challenge and a design opportunity. Read on to see where the journey takes us.

The journey begins.

1 Design

The dream of every design engineer is to come up with the most
beautiful sports motorcycle in the world then turn it into the fastest,
most exclusive, sought after and powerful on the market. This was my
dream too. I wanted to feel the reactions of a racing bike that could
put every available ounce of power through to the ground beneath
me and feel it lean into and hug the curves. I wanted to see perfection
in every single detail of material, shape and efficiency, an example of
mechanical elegance that would be immortal. I wanted a motorcycle
with no half measures, a motorcycle that would combine all of the
technology tried out over years of research, a motorcycle intended for
connoisseurs and true lovers of motorcycles. All of this was my dream.
Today it has come true.

Massimo Tamburini

The 2005 MV Agusta F4 Tamburini is an in-line, four-cylinder, six-
speed, chain-driven motorcycle that can travel from 0 to 60 mph in
3.47 seconds, with a top speed of 190 mph. The entire bodywork is
carbon fibre, including the intake ducts. The overall design reflects
Massimo Tamburini's original masterwork, the Ducati 916. This bike,
of which only 300 were made, retailed at \$42,695. It sold out.[1]

Founded in 1992, Chongqing's Lifan Industry (Group) Co., Ltd
is the largest motorcycle manufacturer in China. (In 2005 China
produced over 17 million motorcycles.)[2] Employing over 8,700
people, Lifan makes motorcycles sold in over 100 countries including Southeast Asia (including Japan), Europe, Africa and South
America, with plant operations in 28 countries. Lifan produces,

among other products, the LF50QT-15. Weighing in at 148 lb, with 48ccs, this single cylinder four-stroke can reach speeds upward of 30 mph.[3]

Which is the *real* motorcycle, the MV Agusta or the 50cc Lifan? Before we can even begin to answer that question we have to ask, what is a motorcycle?

MV Agusta F4 Tamburini, 2005.

Lifan LF50QT-15, 2005.

The Bike

Before the motorcycle came the bicycle. Its forward, propulsive movement results from the transfer of energy from a person's legs to the wheel (originally the front, most often the rear), rather than a motor. The first attempts at bicycle design, however, lacked any means of self-propulsion, requiring instead that the rider push himself and the device forward, using his feet to push off from the ground, first walking then running.[4] Comte Mede de Sirvac's 1791 invention was little more than a wooden bar ending in two forks that held two carriage wheels. Baptized the *cheval de bois* (wooden horse), it inspired a host of more decorative imitations, first called *célérifères* (from the Latin *fero*, meaning to carry, and *celer*, fast) then *vélocifères* after the Revolution.[5] None, however, had any means of steering. In 1817 Karl Friedrich von Drais, a forester and inventor from Mannheim, Germany, devised the first steerable bicycle-like device: he fixed the front wheel to a vertical shaft, allowing the rider to turn left or right, and added a stomach rest to help the rider in propelling the device (which was, like de Sirvac's, made of walnut wood). Conceived primarily as an aid to running, Drais' device enabled its operator to reach the heady speed of 5 to 6 miles an hour, about twice normal walking speed.[6] Called the 'Draisine', it was patented on 5 January 1818 in Baden, and devices modelled on its design became more generally known as velocipedes (from *velox pedis*, swift of foot). But they, too, lacked any means of independent forward propulsion.

A pair of Frenchmen took the next step, giving the rider a means to self-propel the velocipede. In 1861 the father and son French team of Pierre and Ernest Michaux produced what would become the bicycle, a device whereby the rider could employ his or her feet on the front wheel to move forward. In 1855 they had tried fitting

a lever to the wheel, to be powered by the arms, but the design failed owing to balance problems and structural weakness. Then they attached two connecting rods to the front wheel and fastened two large nails (later replaced by a piece of bent tube) to form a foot rest, creating the first pedal. Later models of the 'michaudine' also featured an iron pad to supply friction on the back wheel, the first brake. So successful was their design that they established the first real bicycle industry, 'Michaux et Co.' (later Compagnie Parisienne). Even though these early bikes were soon used for racing, they were still bulky, rigid and heavy, capable of 8 mph at most.

After 1865 the race was on to make the device faster. Englishman James Starley of the Coventry Company made a series of modifications to improve the original velocipede, making it lighter, more durable and more mechanically efficient. In 1879 the ungainly velocipede gave way to a model designed by Harry Lawson, featuring a chain linking pedals to the rear wheel. In the first half of the 1880s, frames adopted a so-called cross shape: a tube ran from the saddle to the pedal wheel and intersected half-way down with another tube connecting the rear wheel to the handlebars. It was elegant and slender but not sufficiently strong or rigid. Englishman Thomas Humber unveiled a diamond-pattern frame at the International Velocipede Exhibition in London in 1866, known as the

Karl Friedrich Drais' 'Draisine', 1817.

'safety' frame because it guaranteed improved stability to the rider. This design was further refined by James Starley's nephew, John Kemp Starley, to produce the Rover Safety bike in 1885. The stability of the safety bike's rigid frame relied on its diamond shape – two triangles connected on what would be the hypotenuse (although it lacked the downtube under the seat seen in modern bicycles). The reliability of this frame relied in turn on the industrial means to produce light, strong metals in a tubular shape.

Sophisticated metallurgical techniques were also required to produce a sturdy but flexible chain that would connect the pedals to the rear wheel, transferring leg power to the rear wheel with sufficient strength to overcome the forces of inertia and friction. Chains were first proposed by Leonardo da Vinci in 1482 and, by the end of the eighteenth century, chains modelled on the pin-and-plate design were employed by mechanical engineers. In 1880 Hans Renold, a Swiss inventor and engineer transplanted in 1873 to England, developed the bush roller chain, a tremendous improvement on the pin-and-plate design. Essentially, the bush roller chain has cylindrical 'rollers' mounted on bushings between inner and outer plates, permitting smooth and reliable weight distribution and movement of the chain around a cog wheel.

Finally, designers had to overcome complaints about the 'bone shaking' experience of riding, devising means of shock absorption for the wheels. While rubber was a natural substance for the outer surface of wheels, the road to usable rubber was a long one. After decades of hapless research, in 1839 Charles Goodyear discovered vulcanization, which combined rubber with chemical substances to make it elastic. Most bicycle manufacturers relied on rubberized strips of cloth nailed to the wheels. However, in 1888, three years after the production of the Rover Safety Bicycle, John Dunlop produced the first pneumatic (air-filled) tyres that could be used for a bicycle. Others contributed to tyre technology, including Giovanni Battista Pirelli (1892), André Michelin (1895), Philip Strauss (1911) and Frank Seiberling (1908). Through the efforts of the Starleys, Renold and Dunlop, we have all the necessary conditions (except for an engine) for the development of the motorcycle.

The diamond-shaped frame provided a natural area to affix a motor – either to the upper transverse bar or, in models subsequent to the Rover, the downtube beneath the seat. Over time, though, motors have been affixed to the rear axle (scooters) and the front wheel as well. The optimum positioning of the engine relies on a number of factors (balance, transfer of power from the engine, relation to other components, etc.), but most designers have placed the engine just ahead of the seated rider and behind the steering column.

Once it occurred to the mechanically inclined to mount a motor onto a bicycle, the question of the identity of the resulting devices remains. For example, Briton Edward Butler mounted a gasoline engine to a vehicle in 1884. However, it had two front wheels and one rear wheel. Car? Motorcycle? Tricycle? Although a gasoline engine propels the vehicle forward, Butler's vehicle is neither an automobile nor a motorcycle. (Sidecar aficionados will note that their motorcycle also has three wheels, further complicating the issue.) In the US Sylvester Howard Roper developed a motorcycle in 1867 (some claim 1869) which, however, was powered by steam, followed in 1868 by Frenchman Louis Guillaume's patented steam engine mounted on a bicycle built by Pierre and Ernest Michaux. Is the source of energy that powers the engine a relevant consideration?

Designing and positioning the engine

Despite the difficulty of defining what we mean by the term 'motorcycle', for many historians German engineers Nicholas August Otto and Gottlieb Daimler share the laurels for creating the first motorcycle. Otto, Daimler's boss, created the engine in 1876, and in 1885 Daimler took this gasoline-powered, four-stroke engine and created the Daimler Einspur, something resembling a torture device with training wheels, named, for reasons obvious to anyone who rode it, the 'Bone Crusher' (the term perhaps a variation on the name for early bicycles, 'bone shakers'). The original flight of the Bone Crusher took place on 10 November in Canstatt, near Stuttgart. Ironically, Daimler never rode his creation – his interest was in testing the engine, not creating a vehicle – leaving that to his colleague Wilhelm Maybach. Daimler himself was no motor-

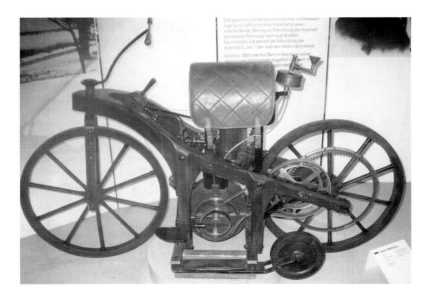

Daimler Einspur, 1885.

cycle enthusiast, seeing the motorcycle as a mere precursor to the more stable, sedate automobile.[7]

A subsequent important development in engine technology came in France, where in 1894 Comte Albert de Dion and Georges Bouton, originally purveyors of steam engines, designed a tricycle with a 125cc engine that, licensed in various European countries and America (and appropriated by many non-licensees), became the standard for motorcycle engines.

The mechanics of internal combustion engines are complicated and, in their details, frequently changing. In early motorcycle design, three elements of engine design are worth noting: ignition, carburation and lubrication.

To achieve the rotational force necessary to propel the motorcycle forward, the engine's piston(s) need to be propelled upward and downward inside the cylinder through a controlled explosion. Depending on the placement of the engine various means can transfer that force to the wheel, causing the motorcycle to move forward. To make the engine crank, one needs a substance that explodes – most commonly a mixture of air and petrol – and an ignition source to cause the explosion. In early engines both the mixing of the fuel–air mixture and igniting it were tricky and often dangerous.

Ignition designs went through three iterations: flame, hot tube and magneto ignition (the latter resulting in spark plug designs common today). In flame ignition, a portion of the cylinder was opened and literally exposed to an open flame, prompting the explosion. This method was obviously dangerous and difficult to control. In hot tube ignition, rather than exposing the fuel–air mixture directly to a flame, a flame heated a tube mounted on the cylinder head. The red hot tube then ignited the fuel–air mixture. Both these methods created problems with timing and, owing to their crudeness, shortened the life of the engine. A magneto system, common in almost all but diesel engines, allowed for a controlled spark that ignites the mixture. One of the reasons for the popularity of the de Dion-Bouton engine was the presence of a battery-and-coil ignition. As in the magneto system it used a spark to ignite the mixture, but it employs an external power source, the battery, rather than an internal flywheel magnet, to do so. (These parallel technologies lasted at least until the early 1960s.) However, even with this more advanced ignition system, care had to be taken to insulate the electrical charge, which could disperse across the metal engine block. Advances in rubber and ceramic insulation were necessary to perfect this technique. Another problem was that, as engine speed increases, the time between ignitions decreases. A solution to this problem was a manual adjustor that controlled the frequency of the sparking.

One factor determining the controlled power of the explosion is the quality of the air–fuel mixture. Ideally, the ratio should be 14.7:1, a ratio known as the Stoichiometric air–fuel ratio,[8] but this was, of course, unknown to early engine designers. The original means to mix air and fuel was through drawing air across an open reservoir of fuel, but an engine in motion disturbed the fuel, making the mixture unreliable. The spray carburettor, which atomized the fuel as it was drawn into the cylinder, was invented by Wilhelm Maybach, a colleague of Gottlieb Daimler. However, Maybach's design did not allow the air–fuel mixture to be easily varied, a necessity for engines that ran at more than one speed. Carl Benz solved this problem through the introduction of the butterfly valve in 1893, allowing for variations in the mixture.

Modern four-stroke motorcycles use either wet or dry sump lubrication, which refers to whether the oil reservoir is part of the engine crankcase or sits outside it. However, early motorcycles,

including the de Dion-Bouton, featured a design with the anxiety-producing name of 'total loss' lubrication system. Oil was fed into the engine through a valve actuated by a hand pump, where it splashed about in the engine, exiting at the bottom via a breather. The speed of the motorcycle determined how often the operator should use the pump. Modern two-stroke engines also used a total loss system, but the oil was mixed with the fuel, and the amount was controlled by a pump activated by the throttle. Nervous or novice riders who pumped too often graced the surrounding area with the acrid smoke of burning oil.

The stability of the motorcycle is an enormous concern. Least stable at low speeds, most stable at high speeds, owing to the gyroscopic effects of the turning wheels, the placement of the engine on the frame is crucial to the motorcycle's stability when starting off and braking. In addition to mountings under the cross bar of the frame and on the downtube, early innovators experimented with all manner of engine placement. The 1900 Cyklon, as well as the

Motosacoche, c. 1910–13.

THE INDIAN

Is the simplest ever made. It has no unnecessary parts to care for, and the necessary parts are so designed as to do the work accurately, perfectly, reliably. That's why *The Indian* has more power for size than anything built. Consult with us.

"LIKE A FLASH"

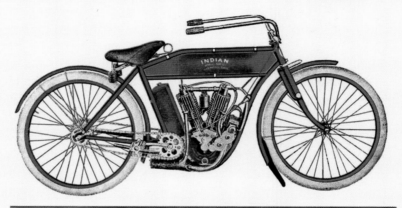

THE INDIAN MOTOCYCLE

J. F. PTACEK'S Motor Shop
390 JACKSON STREET

A Perfect
Machine
Is the
Simplest

Indian with loop frame, 1909.

1909 Cyclo-Tracteur, placed the engine over the front wheel. The 1920s Megola *Zweirad Auto* (two-wheeled automobile) featured the engine cylinders inside the front wheel. In 1901, following a failed attempt four years earlier to mount an engine over the front wheel, Michel and Eugene Werner, Russian exiles working in Paris, experimented with placing the engine lower than in other configurations, between the two wheels.[9] With the bar overhead providing stability, this placement gave the vehicle a much lower centre of gravity than other configurations, providing for greater low speed stability. Further improvement occurred with the fashioning of a loop frame as a cradle for the engine, employed, for example, in early versions of the American Merkel and Harley-Davidson motorcycles.[10] The 1909 Indian solidified the loop frame as superior to the diamond bicycle frame for overall stability and manoeuvrability (though not strength).

Subsequent innovations

By the turn of the century, the concept of the motorcycle as a vehicle distinguished from both the bicycle and the automobile was in place, as was the concept of producing machines for sale. With the increasing volume of motorcycles produced, innovations and improvements were legion. In Belgium FN's designer Paul Kelecom addressed the issue of the painful vibration of motorcycles with his 'self-cancelling' four-stroke engine, in which the paired inner and outer pistons rise and fall inversely, cancelling out much of the vibration. Rather than using belts or chains the FN adopted a shaft drive. Another engine design which both dampened engine vibration and prolonged engine life appeared: the famous horizontally opposed twin boxer engine, not, as is often thought, built by BMW, but by engine designer John Joseph

ANDRE. GRAPPERON

Barter around 1905 for Light Motors Ltd in England, a company later absorbed by the firm that produced Douglas motorcycles.[11]

In the US the Merkel company, home to the famous Flying Merkel, began motorcycle production in 1901–2. In addition to frame innovations, Merkel employed a spring front fork (later to become the standard telescopic front fork), a throttle-controlled oiler, as well as a clever rear suspension (forerunner of the monoshock) that maintained drive train tension.[12]

Not surprisingly, motorcycle production came on the coat-tails of the bicycle, too. Board track bicycle racing was a popular American pastime. In 1900 Swedish-American Carl Oscar Hendstrom constructed a machine for George Hendee, who promoted bicycle races and sold bicycles. The vehicle was intended not for personal transport, but as a pace machine to start bicycle races. However, within a year Hendee and Hendstrom began a company to produce motorcycles commercially, shipping a bike to England to

Board track racer: André Grapperon, of Paris, France.

be exhibited at the 1902 Stanley Bicycle Show. That same year, Hendee and Hendstrom had sold more than 140 motorcycles under the world-famous marque, Indian Motocycles [sic]. Their thin 1908 Indian placed the rider's seat far back on the bike, allowing the rider to spread himself forward over the machine. The slender machine and the rider's posture prompted spectators to give the combo the sonorous name of 'monkey on a stick'. Indeed, as we shall see, racing began as soon as two motorcyclists found themselves next to one another, and mechanical innovations went hand-in-hand with the desire to show the other bloke just how fast your bike could go.

Modern motorcycle design

Generally, modern motorcycles emerge from profit-oriented corporations that employ highly educated designers and engineers

Indian 'monkey on a stick' racer, 1908.

who use complex and sophisticated software and hardware to design, produce and test their new products, which are then handed off to forward thinking marketing departments that study potential consumers with the unwavering attention of a farmer to the weather. A motorcycle in a capitalist economy is decidedly a commodity just like any other. However, like so many products whose existence we take for granted, motorcycles did not originate as sources of potential profit, but were either designed to solve an individual transportation problem or, more likely, were the product of a tinkerer who wanted to see if he could get a bicycle to move under its own steam (or petrol).

The tinkerer, ensconced in his shed, surrounded by tools and parts – which look to the uninitiated like a random collection of metal junk – is a practical person, most comfortable using his hands to shape metal, wood and other materials. For him transforming raw materials into objects of use is a concrete, often trial-and-error process of juxtaposing parts to see what works. The tinkerer fabricates a device from parts. In this respect a transformation occurs between the point at which a practical device is created, and the production of multiple copies of the device for distribution and sale. Once the device *works*, its reliable functioning becomes but one element in considering it as an object for others to use. A one-off device is fine as an object of curiosity, but such a device, considered a prototype, must undergo other, serious considerations. It cannot simply be built; it must now be *designed* and, considered as an object of production, the first distinction arises between design and fabrication.

It is possible to understand the development of motorcycles as a series of solutions to practical mechanical design problems. Theoretically, the motorcycle is a machine whose purpose is propelling human weight forward, subject to two considerations,

those of supporting an engine that can overcome the forces of inertia and friction and, once in motion, of accommodating itself to
the physical forces that act on moving bodies, such as centrifugal
and centripetal forces.

Safety and design

Like bicycles and unlike automobiles, motorcycles are inherently
unstable. If they are not in motion or if at least one of the rider's
feet is not planted firmly on the ground, they tend to topple over.
They are usually smaller than cars, which arguably makes them
less visible. Because the rider mounts, rather than enters, the bike,
the rider lacks the protection of layers of steel that a car operator
enjoys.

Consider some statistics gathered by America's National
Highway Traffic Safety Administration (NHTSA): 'approximately 80
percent of reported motorcycle crashes result in injury or death; a
comparable figure for automobiles is about 20 percent'.[13] Based on
research conducted in 2003, the NHTSA concluded that 'per vehicle
mile traveled . . . motorcyclists were about 32 times more likely than
passenger car occupants to die in a motor vehicle traffic crash and
6 times more likely to be injured'.[14] Whether you are contemplating
riding or have a child anxious to mount a motorcycle, such statistics are arresting.

Naturally, then, there have been design attempts to make motorcycles safer, veering from the strange to the sensible. Rebecca Nul,
the narrator of André Pieyre de Mandiargues' *The Motorcycle* (*La
Motocyclette*, 1963), wears a safety belt, which effectively ties her
to the bike. While a seatbelt may secure a car driver, it would be
a frightening prospect for a motorcyclist to be locked in place during a high-side crash. Automobile safety features more recently

inspired Honda, in 2005, to develop an airbag for its Gold Wing model.[15] Components of motorcycle design, such as 'crash bars', would seem to protect both the engine and the rider's legs in the event of a fall to the side. However, since most crashes (78 percent) occur to the front not the side of a bike, crash bars simply displace injury, usually from the ankle to the shin.[16] Another obvious and traditional approach is to protect the rider's body with clothing. Leather and other artificial materials such as Kevlar have been used to protect the motorcyclist's body, and recently the Hit-Air company began marketing an inflatable jacket, something like a wearable airbag.[17] While the potential for and severity of injury can be ameliorated somewhat, motorcycles remain a relatively dangerous form of transport.

However, statistics also show that single-vehicle motorcycle crashes involve riders who are demographically similar to the automobile accident victim: they are young, unlicenced and/or drunk. Being foolishly impetuous, lacking the necessary vehicular skills or being mentally impaired by drink or drugs leads to crashes of all kinds of vehicles, from power boats to the *Exxon Valdez*. Hence, while motorcycling may be indeed dangerous, statistics mask the fact that accidents most often occur not to the general motorcycle-riding public, but to those who exercise poor judgement. While there will never be a definitive design solution to protect the rider from an automobile blithely turning in front of an oncoming motorcycle, the risks of riding a motorcycle need to be understood in the context of how rider education, sobriety and careful driving dramatically reduce the risks to which motorcycles and their riders are subjected. Designing for safety has inherent limits on motorcycles; we must rely instead on the skill and conscientiousness of the operator.

Purpose-driven design

Once designers have mastered the basic mechanical requirements of the motorcycle, the next and most obvious consideration in motorcycle design is *purpose*. What is the motorcycle *for*? There could be a number of answers to this question. Given the capital necessary for the industrial production of a motorcycle, the initial and obvious answer from the standpoint of the producer is that they are built to *sell*. However, not all producers of motorcycles are focused on sales – consider John Britten of New Zealand, whose wealth enabled him to experiment with various motorcycle designs for years, his only purpose being to design a fast, light V-twin quick enough to beat the Japanese marques dominant in the 1980s and 1990s. So, while we may assume that economic considerations largely drive motorcycle producers, these are not and cannot be their sole purpose.

Clearly when we speak of the purpose of a motorcycle, we are asking what it will be used for by the customer. Racing is an obvious purpose and as noted was central to the technological development of the motorcycle. Not all buyers are racers, however. Many consumers want a reliable form of transportation, one designed to anticipate road and weather conditions, as well as fuel availability. Other riders want a vehicle for work: ease in transporting materials is more important than, for example, the comfort of the vehicle operator. In contemporary culture in the prosperous West, we are seeing another purpose become increasingly important to buyers: they want their machine to dazzle others. From custom choppers to chromed-out cruisers to 186 mph sportbikes, motorcycles also appeal to buyers who already have transportation. Their purpose is to impress their buddies at the pub.

Individuals are not the only buyers of motorcycles. Institutions, in particular governments, have both made and broken motorcycle manufacturers, particularly in time of war. BMWs, Indians, Royal Enfields and Harley-Davidsons – to name only the most prominent – have all played a role in war. With a machine gun mount, armour and a sidecar, a motorcycle built for war sports a distinctive design. Another major source of income and prestige for motorcycle manufacturers is police vehicles. Potential customers can assume that government agencies want power, reliability and cost-effectiveness from their vehicles, values that any individual would endorse as well.

Hildebrand & Wolfmüller, the first company to market a production vehicle successfully, was located in Munich, Germany, at Colosseumstraße 1. Sporting an enormous, water-cooled, two-cylinder 1489cc engine, the Hildebrand & Wolfmüller achieved speeds close to 30 mph. Also notable about this company is that on 20 January 1894 it received German patent number 78553 for a

Hildebrand & Wolfmüller, 1896.

'motorcycle' (*Motorrad*), the first time the term 'motorcycle' was officially employed. Fabulously successful, within three years the company produced several hundred of the machines, and French licensees were also building the bikes. By 1897, however, owing to manufacturing and financial problems, the company collapsed.[18]

The turn of the century saw the proliferation of manufacturing companies throughout Europe and America. However, just as during the Internet boom, within twenty years most of the companies had ceased manufacturing, leaving the field open to only a few marques. While American motorcycles are identified with the brands Indian and Harley-Davidson, in the first decades of the twentieth century over 200 US companies manufactured motorcycles, only to fall quickly victim to market forces. Economic competition among producers clarifies the marketing mind: to design a motorcycle we need to understand what the customer wants to use it for. Failing to properly anticipate and answer this question led to the demise of many marques, and we may assume

A First World War vintage motorcycle machine-gun.

that successful producers have focused on the motorcycle's purpose as the central controlling element in its design.

Race

Designing race bikes assumes central importance among motorcycle manufacturers owing to the dictum that could be applied to vehicles from bicycles to motorcycles to motorcars: race on Sunday, sell on Monday. For the cyclist, racing is a form of competition with other cyclists; for the company, it's a form of competition with other corporations, with the added though brutal benefit (if your bike loses) that racing combines competition with 'free' advertising. From road races such as the Isle of Man Tourist Trophy (TT) to the many international closed tracks of the MotoGP and Superbike, races are a way to test and sell bikes.

Begun in 1907, the Isle of Man TT is the most famous road race in the world. In 1911 the race organizers initiated the now-famous mountain circuit, which was dominated by the US marque Indian, which placed first, second, and third. (This would be the only time an American machine won the race.)[19] The TT, of course, belongs to English and Irish racers, the heyday being the 1960s. Norton dominated the TT and, until 1939, most of European racing. It won 35 TT victories from 1907 to the 1980s with both privateers and teams (featuring, for example, Geoff Duke). Such dominance translated into sales, with young British men hoping to emulate their heroes as they raced their Nortons from café to café against competing BSA Lightnings and Triumph Bonnevilles. Enacting a design impulse of their own, riders themselves created the Triton by dropping a Triumph 650 twin engine into a Norton 'featherbed' frame, an off-the-track dominant café racer that was eventually produced commercially by Dave Degens of Dresda. The Triton found itself in competition with another homespun design, the Norvin, created by introducing a Vincent V-twin into a Norton frame.

The West's confidence in its dominance of motorcycle racing was secure at the beginning of the 1960s, with little to fear from Asia, in particular Japan. Yet motorcycles have had a presence in Japan since their beginning. By 1896 a Hildebrand & Wolfmüller bike had been imported into the country, although over time US manufacturers dominated the import market. In 1909 the home-grown NS appeared, but not until 1924 did the Japanese manu-facturers Rikuo and Murato begin producing domestic motorcycles in quantity. Restrictive trade laws established in 1936 crippled for-eign competition, so it was not until after the Second World War that the Japanese began to distinguish themselves in motorcycle production, beginning with Asahi, Poitner and Showa.[20] Finally,

Dresda Triton, 1968.

by the 1960s, the currently dominant brands of Honda, Kawasaki, Yamaha and Suzuki began to flex their racing muscles.

The death knell for British racing dominance came in 1965 with Yamaha's introduction of the 250cc TD1-B, the third in the TD1 series, and the harbinger of the famous Japanese two-stroke revolution. Lighter, simpler in design (they lack valves) and, perhaps most importantly, firing on every revolution of the piston (rather than every other revolution), two-strokes smoked (both literally and figuratively) the competition. Their fuel inefficiency and shorter life-span, while significant for a commercially distributed vehicle, were much less relevant in the racing sphere. Within the decade, however, Yamaha had produced the TZ75A (early units were 700ccs, with later ones becoming standard 750s), which was both raced and sold commercially. From 1974 to 1982, the TZ750 won every Daytona 200, a phenomenal achievement. (The 1974 winner was the immortal Giacomo Agostini, who that year had jumped from MV Agusta to Yamaha.)[21]

No. 6 Hugh Anderson on a Suzuki 125cc motorcycle on a New Zealand speedway, 1966.

While, for example, MotoGP bikes are race bikes not destined for sale, technological developments in race bikes have historically trickled down to commercially sold units. (Actual race bikes are usually crushed at the end of the season to guard their technological secrets.) For example, much of the technology developed in Yamaha's superbike YZF-R1, a killer at the race track, finds itself in a detuned version, the FZ1, a more sedate but still extremely fast street bike.

Racing bikes are built to go fast. Hence other design considerations, such as longevity, comfort and styling are sacrificed to the god of speed, who is more concerned with power-to-weight and RPM levels. Yet, in paring down all design considerations to a single focus – speed – racing bikes' technological innovations emerge down the production pipeline in commercially produced motorcycles, neatly dovetailing the desire to win with the desire to sell. The street popularity of the Suzuki GSX-R1000 is a testament to the 'race on Sunday, sell on Monday' mantra.

Not all racing occurs on roads. Board track racing, adapted from bicycle racing, was wildly popular early in the twentieth century. (A famous race occurred in America in 1896 pitting 73-year-old Sylvester Roper's steam-powered two-wheeler against bicycles.) Given the repetitive nature of the board track oval and its reliability, racers can eliminate needless weight, such as a braking system.

Not all forms of racing rely on brute speed and handling through curves. Observed trials, an amateur activity, rely on skill in handling (as well as the specialized bike's suspension) with points deducted every time a rider touches his or her foot to the ground. Hill climbing became popular wherever there was a hill and two motorcycles. (There are in fact two distinct events known as hill climbing, one in which motorcycles or cars attempt to reach

Camel cigarette advertisement featuring hill climbing champ, Clem Murdaugh.

the top of a hill or mountain in the shortest amount of time, and another, most popular in the US, where motorcycle riders try to scale a steep hill.) Remaining upright while scaling a vertiginously angled hill requires different design considerations, especially with respect to weight distribution and the nature of the rear wheel and tyre. New Zealand's Burt Munro famously bested rivals by wrapping a rope around his rear tyre to improve traction, others used chains, but tyre designs familiar in off-road vehicles can assist with traction without any modification.

Owing to the power of television and its appeal among children and teenagers, Motocross and its heavily marketed cousin Supercross are now widely popular. Originating in England in 1924 as 'scrambling', renamed 'Motocross' by the Belgians in the 1930s, the sport is conducted on enclosed dirt tracks, enhanced with low dirt rises and sharp turns. Create an artificial circuit inside a sports stadium and you have Supercross. Variations on motocross continue to emerge both in the type and place of racing and the type of machine (all-terrain vehicles, minibikes, etc.). In Motocross and Supercross both two-stroke and four-stroke engines compete, but the design issues focus principally on suspension (the bikes land heavily throughout the race), lightweight construction and responsive brakes. Like other forms of racing, Motocross spawned

Motocross action (featuring Steve McQueen). Still from Bruce Brown's *On Any Sunday* (1971).

commercial versions, the most famous off-road bike being the 1968 Yamaha DT-1. More than any other type, Motocross bikes have been crucial in forming an early attachment to two-wheeled travel, creating new generations of consumers.

Sell

At the other end of the spectrum, motorcycles are also designed to sell as many bikes as possible. If moving units is one's only desire, it makes little sense to actually manufacture them. The 1910 Sears Autocycle is a good example. Sears, for decades a thriving US department store with an equally profitable catalogue business, contracted with the Aurora Machine Company, makers of the Thor motorcycle, and simply slapped a 'Sears' badge onto the petrol tank.

In contrast, consider Danish engineer Jörgen Skafte Rasmussen's company, based in Germany – first in Chemnitz, later in Zschopau – DKW. (DKW stands for *Dampf-Kraft-Wagen*, 'steam-powered vehicle', an early prototype car produced in 1916 by the company.)

Sears Autocycle, 1910.

In 1918 fellow engineer Hugo Ruppe designed a tiny two-stroke toy engine, which Ruppe called '*Des Knaben Wunsch*', 'the boy's dream'. This engine was enlarged and attached to a bicycle, conceived as an 'engine assisted bicycle'. However, so excellent was the design that customers raved about how the engine was capable of ferrying them up mountain roads. Begun as a child's toy, by 1922 over 30,000 of an improved version of the machine had been sold, and '*Das Kleine Wunder*', 'the Little Wonder', enabled DKW to become the largest manufacturer of motorcycles in the world in the 1920s.[22]

In 1946 Soichiro Honda was the 40-year-old owner of a piston factory. After selling his factory to Toyota, he began assembling motorcycles from army surplus parts, and in 1948 founded the Honda Motor Company. Starting in 1949 the company saw success with the production of its Dream D motorcycle and, in 1952, the

Honda Cub, 1958.

Model F Cub, essentially a glorified bicycle with a motor attached.[23] But the *annus mirabilis* for Honda was 1958, with the introduction of the Honda Cub. This tiny 50cc bike, part scooter, part motorcycle, was powered by a four-stroke engine and employed a centrifugal clutch, obviating the need for shifting. Fuel efficient (up to 94 mpg), lightweight, with a step-through chassis design, the Cub was also a tough machine, eminently manoeuvrable through traffic, capable of withstanding abuse and, most importantly, carrying heavy weight, making it an ideal vehicle for urban transport of goods, particularly in Asia. Currently manufactured in fourteen countries (primarily in Southeast Asia) and exported to over 160, with sales of well over 35 million, the Honda Cub is the best selling motorcycle in history. In the 1980s the engine capacity was doubled to 100ccs, and Honda Wave (or NF), introduced in 1995, added further refinements to the frame. Alongside the Model-T Ford and the Volkswagen Beetle, the Honda Cub remains

Honda motorcycle factory in Japan, 1981.

an icon, the most widely distributed and influential motorcycle in transportation history.

Transport/Work/War

Since their inception motorcycles have been employed for practical tasks: the transport of goods, the policing of communities and as instruments of war. The 1925 Harley-Davidson JD was quickly adapted to the delivery of goods. One imported to Australia, for instance, was used to deliver cookies in New South Wales, with the storage box affixed in place of a sidecar. As early as 1909 Arthur Davidson established contact with the Rural Mail Carriers of America Association, achieving a link between motorcycles and mail delivery.[24] From early in the twentieth century until today, using motorcycles in a work environment has enabled young men and women to make money, and to do so with some style and excitement.

1925 Harley-Davidson JD brings biscuits to Aussies.

The Maserati automobile company's sister firm, a producer of spark plugs, acquired Italmoto of Bologna, and by 1953 they were producing motorcycles. A superb example of the motorcycle as work vehicle is the Ciclocarro, a 50cc, three-speed two-stroke with a truck bed. In Tokyo's 2004 Motor Show the 'Working Motorcycle Zone' displayed contemporary small-engine two-wheelers that had been adapted to perform specific tasks, from pizza delivery (with 'special capabilities to maintain food temperature'), to newspaper delivery (with baskets to carry newspapers, as well as shields to protect the cargo from inclement weather), to bikes designed to assist in vehicle breakdown repair on the road.[25] Despite advances in motorcycle design and technology – making them faster and sleeker – a place remains worldwide for bikes that are cheap to operate, simple to repair and dependable, despite inclement weather. No better example of such work vehicles can be imagined than the Piaggio 'Ape' ('AH-pay', Italian for 'bee').

Maserati Ciclocarro, 1958.

Italy, like much of the rest of Europe, was devastated by the Second World War both physically and economically. As individuals suffered, so did large businesses, and the aeronautics industry – so tied to warfare – was particularly affected. Founded in 1882, Piaggio had been involved in many industries – timber, producing shipping components, railway car construction and, in Pontedera, aircraft engines. With their Pontedera facility almost completely destroyed in 1944, in 1945–6 the gifted aeronautical engineer Corradino D'Ascanio, charged with coming up with a new product for the company to sell, designed the Vespa (Italian for 'wasp'), which by 1953 was to sell over 500,000 units and remains today not only an attractive and reliable motor scooter, but an icon of glamour, freedom and fun.[26] In D'Ascanio's words, 'the creation of a modern means of transport, with the popularity of a bicycle, the performance of a motorbike, the elegance and comfort of an automobile, is now reality'.[27] The company has sold 50 million Vespas over six decades, cornering the market in Italy, and exporting to Greece, Germany, the US, France and Australia.[28] To this day D'Ascanio's debt to aeronautics can be seen in the Vespa's distinctive single-tube front fork with off-set wheel, modelled after an aeroplane's landing gear.

Introduced in 1948, the Vespa 125 was designed with rear suspension, along with a metal rack on the back, aiding workers who needed to transport goods. (The 1953 125U or 'utilitaria' was a stripped down version for work.)[29] Also in 1948, Piaggio modified its scooter design, producing the Ape. While sporting three wheels, mechanically the vehicle employed virtually the same components as the Vespa. Produced in a number of styles on a semi-monocoque frame, this two-seater began with a 50cc motor, but has evolved into a number of different forms, using a 395cc or 492cc diesel engine.[30] Manufactured in India under contract from Piaggio by

Bajaj Auto with a 150cc engine, the Ape is the worldwide vehicle of choice for reliable work transportation.

Warfare makes even more demands on a motorcycle than work, as the example of Germany shows. Germany holds pride of place in motorcycle history as the originator of the first internal-combustion-driven motorcycle and home to the first motorcycle production company. By the beginning of the First World War, in Germany alone there were 55 motorcycle production companies.[31] The German army displayed an interest in motorcycles as early at 1902 (testing an NSU Type A), and the firms Victoria, Wanderer and NSU all sought to be the military's motorcycle outfitter. In 1904 NSU supplied Wilhelm Kohler with a single-cylinder NSU machine, making him the first motorized dispatch rider in the German military. While there was a push to employ motorcycles in the First World War, the Germans were beset by the problem of bad roads that were little more than mud slides – particularly on the Eastern front – making horses (the '*Hafermotoren*' or 'oat engines') more reliable.[32]

In fact, the first 'Yank' to enter Germany in the First World War did so on a Harley-Davidson. Roy Holz was driving an

German war bikes at work.

The first Yank and Harley to enter Germany. 11/11/18

officer in his sidecar in northern Belgium on 11 November 1918. Owing to bad weather Holz became disoriented and entered Germany, where he was captured. Three days later, after the Armistice, Holz and his passenger were released, only to become lost again as they headed east. Once they realized their error, they headed back west. While it was a wrong turn, rather than a triumphal entry, a motorcyclist was the first to enter Germany, three days early![33]

In the run up to the Second World War Hitler established the paramilitary Nationalsozialistische Kraftfahrerkorps (NSKK), the 'motorized power of the [Nazi] party'. One member who later rose to prominence was Franz Josef Strauss, former Minister President of Bavaria. Motorcycles were present during the 1933 party meeting in Nuremburg.[34] For messenger and training purposes BMW R4 and R35 bikes were used, and R11 and R12 models, outfitted with sidecars, were used for rapid transit. While commercial production

'The First Yank and Harley to Enter Germany'.

of motorcycles was diverted to the Lightning War by 1941, the inadequacy of civilian machines had been established. Zündapp and BMW developed special war machines, the KS 750 and the R 75 respectively. Zündapp produced 18,635 machines for the war effort, while BMW produced 16,545.[35] The BMW was based on specifications submitted by the German Army and featured a 'side-car wheel drive, a locking differential, cross-country and reverse gears, a felt air filter, a new chassis, off-road tires and excellent handling'. Further modifications produced a bike that could haul more than 880 pounds.[36] These machines were particularly successful in negotiating the difficult terrains of the African campaign and the Russian front.

One of the more diverting examples of wartime motorcycle design was Royal Enfield's 'Flying Flea', a two-stroke, lightweight 125cc bike built by Royal Enfield for a Dutch concessionaire of DKW, beginning in 1938 after the Germans cancelled their contract. Royal Enfield Designer Ted Pardoe, on the instructions of the Dutch, reverse engineered a DKW RT. A tubular steel cage was built to transport the Flea, not only by aircraft, gliders and tanks, but also for dropping it into the front lines with airborne forces. While the majority of motorcycles built by Royal Enfield were 346cc machines based on already existing models (55,000 were built), the Flea provides an interesting example of wartime motorcycle design.[37] (After the war, the Flea became known as the RE125.) The Triumph was similarly used successfully by the British on the Western front, and its popularity with soldiers no doubt led many, after the war, to avail themselves of Army surplus bikes.

Motorcycles have also been used in times of peace by law enforcement. By 1911 the city of Berkeley, California, had a Police Motorcycle Patrol. Harley-Davidsons were used by Japanese police as early as 1923. Speedy and able to weave through snarled traffic, motorcycles have been valued by police departments all over the world, despite the relatively high percentage of officer fatalities. (Motorcycles ranked third as the most frequent cause of death among American policemen in the twentieth century.)[38] Indians, such as the 1940 Indian Four, were popular with police departments, but the 1925 Henderson De-Luxe was favoured over both the Harley-Davidson and the Indian owing to its smooth running and speed. In England the 1948 Triumph Speed Twin had many adherents, though by 1960 the Velocette L.E. was the most favoured urban vehicle, owing to its near silent operation. In Germany the 1953 BMW R67/2 was the choice of the Highway Patrol. Indeed, BMW would seem to be the motorcycle of choice for law enforcement, and they have the largest market share in law enforcement worldwide. Despite its higher cost, the BMW's reliability, relatively inexpensive operating expenses and, most important, its much vaunted ABS braking system make it cost effective and safe over the long run. However, despite the exit of Kawasaki (the KZ1000) from the police cruiser market, in recent years BMW has seen its market share fall, particularly in Europe.

Dazzle

To ride a motorcycle is to be able to fly along the ground, and the ongoing thrill that a motorcycle provides is essentially visceral and, as many motorcyclists would claim, incommunicable: to experience a motorcycle you have to ride one, preferably as fast as possible. However, even to the non-initiate, motorcycles have an innate visual appeal. Elegant or brutal, sinuous or blocky, the motorcycle, unlike other transportation devices, displays its technology for all to see (unless it is shrouded under fairings). With little other than an engine,

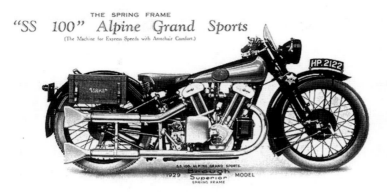

THE SPRING FRAME
"SS 100" Alpine Grand Sports
(The Machine for Express Speeds with Armchair Comfort.)

Illustration shows optional fitting of Gear Box Control.   Forward position as shown on opposite page is standard.

PRICE, with Magdyno Lighting, Electric Horn, Ammeter, Rear Wheel driven Jaeger Speedometer, Licence Holder, Propstand, Aluminium Number Plates, Permanent Rear Folding Footrests, etc., etc.   -   **£180**

(Extra for Dual Head Lamps and Large Pannier Bags, as shown in illustration, see page 10)

2

two wheels and a seat, the motorcycle is the possibility of motion stripped down to its essence, and that purity is part of its appeal.

Also, it often sports a lot of shiny chrome.

The Brough (pronounced 'Bruff') Superior is one of the most beautiful motorcycles ever built. The Nottingham works of George Brough produced a series of bikes from 1919 to 1940. The hand built 'Rolls-Royce of motorcycles' is probably best known as T. E. Lawrence's bike of choice, and the one on which he was fatally injured. Lawrence owned seven Broughs, and named each Boanerges ('son of Thunder'). He spoke rapturously of the sensation of motorcycle riding in his memoir of military service, *The Mint*:

> A skittish motor-bike with a touch of blood in it is better than all the riding animals on earth, because of its logical extension of our faculties and the hint, the provocation, to excess conferred by its honeyed untiring smoothness. Because Boa loves me, he gives me five more miles of speed than a stranger would get from him.[39]

Brough Superior SS100 Alpine Grand Sports, 1930.

Lawrence's endorsement, combined with their exclusiveness, made Broughs legendary.

If the Brough was the Rolls-Royce, the Crocker was the 'Duesenberg' of motorcycles, the preeminent bike in America prior to the Second World War. It was the brainchild of Albert Crocker, who had worked for the Aurora Automatic Machine Company, maker of Thor motorcycles, and then for Indian, before embarking on his own plan to design a 'superbike'. Only 75 or so were built between 1936 and 1940, each hand built to order out of parts cast in Crocker's Los Angeles workshop. Advertisements claimed, 'every Crocker motor is a bench job'.[40] The bikes also featured cast aluminium gas tanks, large dashboards and decorative tail lights prized by custom builders to this day. Their bold aesthetic design was matched by their performance: with their 1000cc engine, they could cruise at 90–100 mph. Crocker backed his machine's

Brough Superior ridden by Eric Fernibough to set a world speed record, 1938.

performance with a guarantee to return the full purchase price if the buyer was beaten by a factory Harley-Davidson or Indian. He never had to make good on his offer.

Founded in 1912, Aermacchi (short for Aeronautica Macchi, a maker of seaplanes), turned to motorcycle production after the Second World War. They designed a series of light, fast motorcycles, setting speed records along the way. Designer Alfredo Bianchi, formerly of Alfa Romeo and Parilla, was brought into the fold in 1956 as technical director. He produced the Aermacchi Chimera 175 (the 'dream'), based on drawings of 'the ultimate motorcycle' by Italian car designer Count Revelli. The bike was advertised as stylishly up-to-the minute: '*la moto fuoriserie con la linea di domani*', 'the motorcycle specially built in contemporary style'. The totally enclosed styling actually looks forward to today's fully faired bikes, but the engine design was retro, using pushrods instead of overhead cams. Note as well the unusual frame, a single-tube design. Revelli's 'dream' was too futuristic for its time, however, and even a competing version by Parilla, the Slughi 99 ('Desert Greyhound'), which offered an optional windshield, failed with consumers.

In terms of sheer mass and eye-popping visual design, nothing in contemporary motorcycle design can match the Honda Rune. First built in 2004, based on the Valkyrie, the Rune somehow combines massiveness with elegance. This 8-feet single-seater features an aluminum frame, and is a testament to the willingness of a huge international corporation (the bike was manufactured in Marysville, Ohio) to take the risk of producing an expensive bike with radical design features. The company's brashness is reflected in a statement released as the bike was unveiled, 'We can design and build anything better than anyone else.'

In addition to corporate-led designs, contemporary boutique designers are making impressive strides. The Geneva-based Osmos company is a good illustration. Designer and entrepreneur Dominique Mottas 'reinvented the wheel' by creating a rotating bearing attached to the rim of a wheel, ridding the wheel of spokes

Aermacchi Chimera 175.
Valkyrie Rune, 2004.

and a centre bearing. Patented in 1990, this hubless wheel has, according to Osmos, applications to all wheeled vehicles, from motor-cycles to railroad equipment.[41]

The whole enchilada

As we have seen, design of purpose-built bikes emphasizes certain capacities of motorcycles while de-emphasizing others. For example,

Osmos hubless wheel system, photograph by Anoush Abrar, *Intersection* magazine.

in a quest for speed, rider comfort is secondary. Motorcycles built for warfare sacrifice acceleration to the weight of armour. Any design directed by a specific purpose will emphasize certain potentialities of the bike while neglecting others. However, some bikes have managed to both fulfil their purpose and satisfy the expectations of a wider customer base. For a bike of this nature, we could ask a series of questions, among them, how well does the bike fulfil the function for which it was designed? Does the bike incorporate novel technology, or employ traditional technology in a novel way? Is the bike aesthetically pleasing? Is the bike popular with the buying public? While no bike can fulfil all these categories to their limits (a bike might have cutting edge technology, but sell only moderately well, or it might be wildly popular and attractive, but incorporate design elements already found on other bikes), we can say that a significant number of bikes possess the 'whole enchilada'.

Rollie Free setting a speed record at the Bonneville Salt Flats in 1948 on a Vincent HRD Black Lightning wearing only a bathing suit and swim cap.

Some bikes fulfilling these criteria have already been mentioned. For example, the wildly popular Honda Cub's combination of dependability, simplicity, economy and adaptability make it one of the best motorcycles in history, despite its lack of size and speed. The Norton Manx, with its race-track dominance, superior handling and coveted frame, not only was popular, but also spawned the Dominator as well as the home-built Tritons and Norvins. What follows is a representative sample of motorcycles that seem to have everything.

For a combination of speed and elegant appearance, few motorcycles can match Vincents. Philip Vincent, after acquiring the HRD trademark in 1928 and hiring Australian engineer Phil Irving in 1931, began producing a line of motorcycles, most notably the Rapide in 1936. However, the marque acquired worldwide fame in 1948 with the Vincent Black Lightning, a big twin which could cruise at speeds over 100 mph.[42] In September of that year Rollie Free set a record of 150 mph on a Lightning at America's Bonneville Salt Flats in Utah. The bike inspired musician Richard Thompson to pen 'Vincent Black Lightning'. The heavier Black Shadow was essentially the same bike as the race-ready Lightning, fast, black and beautiful. Dr Hunter S. Thompson immortalized his love for the vehicle in his fiction and gonzo journalism.[43]

Ducati motorcycles are synonymous with speed, technological innovation (most famously, their Desmodromic valve control) and stylishness. Dr Fabio Taglioni was responsible for Ducati's novel engine designs, his numerous innovations stretching across a career that lasted 50 years. The 1972 750SS V-twin established Ducati as a racing force to reckon with, as well as a builder of powerful bikes that bonded customers to the company's products. The mere reference to Ducati's desmodromic heads sends owner and writer Ted Bishop into Keatsian raptures, 'Desmo, Desmo, the very

The larger context

In the absence of a national mandate, such as that of ancient Rome, reliable roads for transport of people and goods have always been problematic. Dependable and inexpensive materials for road surfaces that resist climatic stresses are relatively new. Hence, in designing a motorcycle, road surface has to be taken into consideration: are there existing roads? Are they dirt, gravel, bitumen or concrete? Will the motorcycle be run on a track, on a superhighway, on a mountain trail or on a combination of these surfaces? Might these roads experience ice, flooding, sand or mud?

Topography and its influence on weather is another obvious consideration. Motorcycles designed for flat areas have little need for the torque required to climb hills. The placement of the engine could become relevant in areas where streams periodically cross

Riders of both sexes display the latest Indian models outside P C Price Cycle Importer, Stratford, New Zealand, c. 1915.

roads. Radical changes in temperature owing to changing altitudes might result in carburation problems. Excessively hot climates may tax lubrication and cooling systems that cannot withstand extreme engine heat.

Distances, limited by topography or by national boundaries, are also a consideration. A small, island-bound country such as Japan has no need for 2000cc cruisers. Riders in tightly circumscribed urban areas benefit from small, quick machines such as scooters. Large countries with extensive highway systems, such as the US, require motorcycles with substantial gas tanks, comfortable seating and large engines. Countries with a variety of road systems, such as New Zealand, require motorcycles outfitted with multi-purpose tyres, lower-engine shielding and reinforced shock absorption.

How one designs a motorcycle also depends on cultural considerations. Muslim countries that deny women the right to drive have little need to attend to the biological and cultural factors associated with women riders. Despite the masculinist orientation of motorcycle riding in Western countries since the end of the Second World War, in countries such as England and the US motorcycles were marketed to women as well as men for decades. Women's shorter stature, relative lack of upper body strength, and fashion choices all bear on how a motorcycle should be designed in such cultures. The step-through design of scooters led Italian priests, owing to their flowing vestments, to adopt them for transportation, giving rise to an unintended cultural association. In cultures where riders are men who ride for recreation, increasing the opportunities for riders to customize the bike by changing exhausts, handlebars and modifying the engine should be considered during the design stage. The ubiquitous worldwide presence of Hollywood films has led to consumer desire for bikes just like Brando's in *The Wild One*, or a chopper resembling the Captain America bike in *Easy Rider*.

While environment is certainly a factor in motorcycle design, the economic system in which motorcycles are designed is equally relevant. A prosperous economy, such as many of those in the West, produces a number of unintended consequences, among them urban concentrations of relatively underpaid workers. This working class may go on to create a middle class, but both working and middle classes exist as large horizontal markets of people who share similar buying capacity, economic aspirations and daily transportation needs. Some countries have developed public transportation systems to accommodate their working populations while some, like the US (other than in exceptional locales such as New York and Chicago), have not. Hence, the motorcycle designer in a capitalist society, recognizing that selling more units at a lower price is a key to success, adjusts his or her design accordingly. Given that capitalism also creates a small wealthy class, other designers can concentrate on 'custom' designs of bikes for those with deep pockets.

Other factors influence both design and marketing of motorcycles, such as the rising price of petrol, which might drive otherwise automobile-oriented customers toward more fuel-efficient vehicles. Increasing automobile traffic in large urban areas, such as emerging economic hot spots in China, creates unending lines of automobiles, prompting customers to abandon four wheels for the more nimble two-wheeler.

Another feature of relatively open capitalist societies is the ability of gifted individuals, aided by patent protections, to create devices that transform their society, from Alexander Graham Bell and the Wright Brothers, to Steve Wozniak and Steve Jobs. The tinkerer has been a clearly defined social role, from Leonardo da Vinci to Thomas Edison. The early design developments in motorcycles, in England, France, Germany and the US all originated with one or more isolated tinkerers.

Successful economies provide easy access to goods and services. In designing a bike for a particular market, external economic considerations become important factors influencing bike design. Consider some of the following questions:

If the motorcycle is gasoline-powered, where will the fuel come from? One can fill the tank with fuel at home or a nearby supply point, but is there a reliable chain of supply stations for fuel along routes motorcyclists might take? In the absence of this, is the device worth producing? (The same considerations obtain today with ethanol-based vehicles.)

Is there a reliable supply of metal, rubber and parts for the fabricator? Is there social unrest in the country that supplies rubber? Are there legislative moves to enact tariffs that would restrain the importation of steel? Are disputes breaking out in the family-owned parts supply firm, following the death of the family patriarch?

Will road conditions and other competing vehicles (horse carts, automobiles) share the road with the vehicle? From the beginning of motorcycling, the devices have been considered noisy, dangerous and frightening to horses and other travellers. (In 1811 in Milan the Director General of Police prohibited riding velocipedes at night, owing to their danger to pedestrians.)[47]

Are financial resources sufficient, in the case of either cash or loans, to sustain the production through times of rising material costs or falling customer demand? Around the world marques have disappeared not because they didn't produce a competitive product, but owing to financial issues.

Does the design dovetail with the needs of the economy in which the motorcycle is produced? One of the reasons for the spectacular success of the Vespa was its position within a road-rich but impoverished post-war population. As in Germany following the First World War, motorcycles depended for their success on their positioning within a battered economy, lacking a universal public transportation system that encouraged individual entrepreneurism, which in turn relied on individuals being able to move from the home to the workplace.

As these and many other considerations suggest, it's not enough to produce a mechanically reliable, inexpensive motorcycle. Forces far outside the control of the motorcycle producer must be considered during the design phase and, if they are not, these forces may well threaten the integrity of the production process.

Taken together, these factors explain why the West initiated development of the motorcycle (even though in the contemporary world India and the countries of Asia are the largest consumers of motorcycles). Europe and the US took the lead in the transition to motorcycles, no doubt owing to responsive industrial economies capable of processing the raw materials of rubber and metal, cultures given over to mechanical tinkering, capitalist urbanization requiring workers to move to and from the workplace and the general, though modest, increase in affluence among the working class. This enabled them to own private means of transport, namely bicycles, which were then adapted to leisure and sporting activities. Until these economies enabled the mass production of vehicles and consequent price reductions, emphasizing volume production over comfort or luxury, agricultural societies such as those of Asia were not in a position to take advantage of these emerging forms of transport that gave working individuals greater autonomy.

The spread of the bicycle and motorcycle to less developed societies was, of course, inevitable, as manufacturers sought out new markets. Like the contemporary example of the cell phone in underdeveloped economies such as those of central Africa, introducing a novel technological device into a struggling economy can have remarkable and sometimes unpredictable consequences.

The rural fisherman who can now speed his catch to market on a motorcycle can eliminate middlemen, provide fresher product to customers, gain greater economic autonomy, provide heretofore unavailable opportunities to his family, such as education, and generally put himself in a position to be a more active participant in local economic and political interactions. At the same time, novel transportation devices can also introduce inequalities into communities, upsetting the traditional reciprocal dependency of people and families in favour of more independent 'modern' individuals, whose success can engender disruption of the social and economic fabric of a village.

Design in transition

The development of motorcycle design resulted from an already successful transportation device, the safety bicycle, being married with the developing mechanical technologies of steam and internal combustion power. Steam, although not needing refined fuel, gave way to the more complex but (relatively) efficient internal combustion engine. This transition to motorcycles, automobiles and industrial devices requiring hydrocarbon-based power has transformed the global economy and the surface of the earth – now crisscrossed by road systems – and resulted in countless international conflicts, continuing today, regarding control of the resources to produce fuel for engines. While the earth and human welfare have been significantly harmed by the development of the internal combustion engine – beginning (and perhaps ending) with global warming – human life has also been made more comfortable, various and ultimately happier by developments in transportation technology. Alternate technologies to the internal combustion engine have been proposed and tested (fuel cell, electric engines, hybrids, hydrogen),

but interesting environmental improvements to internal combustion engines have also been explored. In particular, the Homogeneous Charge Compression Ignition seems to have promise. This design seeks to marry the best features of diesel and spark-ignition engines, resulting in better fuel efficiency (an improvement over traditional gasoline engines) and fewer pollutants (an improvement over traditional diesel engines). The Honda AR two-stroke motorcycle engine improved fuel efficiency by 27 per cent and reduced hydrocarbon emissions by more than 50 per cent, compared with a traditional two-stroke. Despite improvements in emission reduction, work still needs to be done this area.[48]

The motorcycle, in particular, while aiding the proletariat in their transportation needs in the West and helping with transport in

Brigade Street, Bangalore, India.

Western countries recovering from the economic devastation wrought by war, has had perhaps its most profound effect in developing economies, where decentralized, individually based production of goods and services has been helped by the motorcycle's ability to transport goods in a timely fashion. This is not to say that, for example, concentration on racing technology is a pastime of the idle, wealthy, consumer societies of the West, since those technologies create improvement in production machines that find their way to motorcycles around the world. The migration of Western motorcycle production facilities, such as Royal Enfield to India or Zündapp to China, has sparked and will continue to provoke a series of improvements that respond to local needs: bikes may need to be made less expensive, or more fuel efficient, or employ local fuel resources (e.g. Brazil's current success with converting sugar cane to fuel for engines). These developments will in turn find their way back to the West. The Indian concern of Bajaj Auto is instructive. Beginning in the late 1940s to import foreign-made motorcycles, in 1959 it received a government licence to produce bikes and by 1970 had produced over 100,000 two- and three-wheelers. In 1991 Bajaj and Kawasaki joined design forces to produce a number of bikes, including the Kawasaki Bajaj Eliminator, India's first homegrown cruiser. Today, in addition to a large home market, Bajaj exports to over 50 countries including the US and Europe.[49] In motorcycle markets globalization has occurred, though not unilaterally from West to East and South. Instead we find that markets interpenetrate one another.

Despite the foregoing presentation, it is also important to note that while motorcycle design is evolutionary, creating improved designs based on previous ones, it is also recursive: we find the original engine-bolted-onto-a-bike designs recurring when the environment and economic conditions are right (e.g. the introduction of the American Whizzer in the 1940s, a bike with an engine attached). As the price of petrol spirals upward, we may see designers looking backward, not forward, for solutions in motorcycle design. What is clear is that we are not at the end of motorcycle design, with our carbon fibre 185+ mph sportbikes, but at a moment of transition.

2 | Identity

The social arrangements of agricultural economies centre on the family, who either work a family farm or are in the employ of a landowner. The horse that draws the plough can also pull the wagon that carries the family or its agricultural products to the village centre for barter or storage. For the highly unusual journey to a city, a coach might be available. With the advent of urbanization, however, modern transport devices were designed to carry disparate groups of unrelated people, via horse-drawn carriages, railroads, aeroplanes and cars.

The motorcycle, by contrast, will carry at most two people (without a sidecar). The urban worker astride his motorcycle carries nothing but his skills to the workplace. The motorcycle owner finds himself reflected in the choice and appearance of his vehicle. Unlike modes of transport that physically enclose the person – such as a bus or an automobile – the motorcycle places its rider as well as itself on display in a melding of person and motorized machine unlike any other. The urban worker at the workplace, surrounded not by his family but by men and women of his own age, finds in his motorcycle an opportunity for self-definition.

Of course, an individual seeks self-definition not only to separate himself from members of his group; he also seeks a group that

The motorcycle as a gathering point: from the Maori community, New Zealand, c. 1920 to . . . the Motor Maid 'family' in Orlando, Florida, 1999.

will mirror his own sense of self. Like choices in fashion, loyalty to sporting clubs or membership in bowling leagues, the selection of a motorcycle establishes one's identity both as an individual and as a member of a group.

The possibilities for group association are many. Motorcyclists can join groups based on the motorcycle marque such as the Honda Riders Club or the Harley Owners Group. Clubs form around 'classic' bikes, with the focus on collecting or racing. In a specific geographic locale, clubs can form around their own concerns, like a racing or touring club. They can form around a specific type of bike, such as scooters (e.g. Vespa and Lambretta groups) or sportbikes. Clubs can organize members of a particular nation-state, such as the American Motorcycle Association (AMA), or a region, such as FEMA, the Federation of European Motorcyclists' Associations, or internationally, such as FIM, the Fédération Internationale de Motocyclisme.

Mr and Mrs Willie Kay on their Indian Tricar, c. 1906.

Organizations can be formed to pursue particular political agendas of riders, such as Motorcycle Rights Organizations (MROs). Clubs can limit their membership to persons of a particular gender or sexual orientation, such as the Women's International Motorcycle Association or Dykes on Bikes. Clubs can form around a specific kind of riding from racing to endurance to stunt riding.

Clubs such as these exist worldwide. They exist so that like-minded people can pursue a common interest and advance their own individual concerns through the strength of a community, gaining a sense of belonging and personal identity in the process. In the popular mind, however, motorcyclists aren't collegial fellow citizens who bolster their sense of community by joining the local motorcycle club. Motorcyclists are deviants.

This image of the motorcyclist as somehow a social outsider (who socializes with other outsiders) is an international post-Second World War phenomenon. The US takes the lead in popular consciousness with its motorcycle 'gangs' such as the Hells Angels, but groups in other cultures are treated as deviant as well, with interesting differences owing to the culture in which they become manifest. Mods and Rockers, their public display infused with self-

Massed motorcycles at Venice, California, c. 1910.

regarding class consciousness, are an enduring image in British popular culture. Nowhere, however, do we find a more colourful and public dramatization of social disaffection than in the Japanese 'kamikaze bikers', the *bosozoku*.

The blessing of the bikes by a Christian motorcycle community.

Bosozoku

The *bosozoku* are groups of Japanese youths who engage in theatrical, high-speed urban motorcycle riding, accompanied by automobiles. Unsurprisingly, they are simultaneously considered dangerous delinquents and romantic risk-takers, depending on the source of the description. While motorcycle clubs existed early on in post-war Japan, it wasn't until the 1970s that they became targets of public and media concern. Tokyo police first recorded a gathering of *kaminari* (thunder tribes) – the original name of the *bosozoku* – at the Mejii Shrine on 4 September 1959. While *bosozoku* groups remain active to this day, the period from 1979 to 1981 is considered to be their heyday.[1]

The *bosozoku* spend weekend evenings driving on urban streets at twice the legal limit and three times the speeds most drivers can hope to achieve in Japan's urban congestion.[2] Their dedication to speed is at the heart of their name, an amalgam of three characters (*Bo-So-Zoku*): *Bo* stands for *violent* and *So* for racing, while *Zoku* is a common ending to Japanese words describing social units, and in particular youthful groups (e.g. *taiyo-zoku* or 'sun tribe', one of the first post-war manifestations of Japanese youth culture). The common English translations all emphasize speed: the *bosozoku* are 'kamikaze bikers', 'lightning tribes', 'thunder tribes' or simply 'speed tribes'. In simplest terms, the *bosozoku* are a group of highly visible young men (and a few young women) who engage in structured, high-speed riding along major urban thoroughfares, such as Kawaramachi Avenue in Kyoto, while wearing theatrical costumes.

In their pursuit of speed they can be seen as the precursors to contemporary US sportbike riders zigzagging at high speeds on the nation's congested highways or gathering in the wee hours of the morning to perform wheelies and acrobatic moves on less congested

city streets. In their intention to shock and awe spectators, from among their group or onlooking *ippanjin* (ordinary citizens), they appear seemingly no different from the iconic image of the motorcyclist as rebel, Asian versions of the Hells Angels or Outlaws. Like their American counterparts accused of acts of criminal conspiracy, a minority of *bosozoku* members have become associated with the Yakuza, Japan's organized crime syndicate.

But significant differences separate the *bosozoku* from other motorcycle organizations – present and past. *Bosozoku* members have traditionally ridden smaller bikes, generally 250 to 400ccs, unlike the lumbering Harleys of American clubs. Since Japan has historically restricted sales of motorcycles above 750ccs, these are considered mid-sized bikes.[3] They are heavily decorated with brand-name accessories and sport unbaffled pipes, with the resultant deafening roar.

At its peak *bosozoku* riding was undeniably dangerous, with almost 180 youths killed in the years 1980–1, injuries in the 2,000

29 *Bosozoku* with bike.

range, and arrests for dangerous driving amounting to over 6,700.[4] The seeming indifference to this danger can be ascribed to the universal sense of youthful immortality and the intense emotional rewards of skilfully driving a motorcycle at high speeds while attracting the admiring and critical attention of hundreds of observers.

While many motorcyclists dismiss automobiles as 'cages' driven by civilians, automobiles are an essential part of *bosozoku* culture. Upwards of 60 per cent of the vehicles on their *shinai boso* (organized rides) are tricked out automobiles.[5] The most recent instalment of *The Fast and the Furious*, subtitled *Tokyo Drift* (2006), features a *bosozoku* group, but motorcycles barely make an appearance. Off the screen, the motorcyclists, in fact, often sacrifice themselves as protection for 'cagers'. Motorcyclists at the back of the pack engage in *ketsumakuri* (tail wagging) to keep the police at bay, falling further back and zigzagging until the larger pack of vehicles is a safe distance away.

The *bosozoku* are also distinct in their overt acknowledgement that participation in such activities is a consequence of adolescence, a temporary stage that they not only expect but are forced to conclude. Members are expected to 'graduate' from motorcycles to cars by the age of eighteen, even if they do not yet have a driver's licence, or face ridicule.[6] In a sense, then, participation is a rite of passage rather than a rehearsal of or preparation for adult self-presentation.

Membership in the *bosozoku* also entails a degree of affluence that sets them apart from other youth subcultures (with the exception perhaps of the Mods). Products of an advanced economy, Japanese youths of the 1980s, in particular, had disposable income and leisure time, for they were not expected to work. They lavished their extra cash on decorating their small bikes with accessories.

But there was – and still is – no pride of place reserved for 'rat bikes' or DIY ingenuity. Instead, performance is secondary to the conspicuous display of brand-name parts. Tank colours, decorative mirrors and flashing lights are chosen with no concern for function but purely for aesthetics. The horns, along with the favoured handlebar configuration – *shibori* – with the bars bent rakishly back toward the rider, make this obvious. As important as the vehicle is the public appearance of the *bosozoku* rider. Just as the utilitarian motorcycle is transformed into a decorative object, riders modify standard versions of working clothes to create elaborately decorated and embroidered costumes.

In his riding a *bosozoku* enacts the hypermasculine values associated with the samurai. The common names for their uniforms similarly convey masculinity and aggression. Two of the more outrageous 'looks' are the *tokkofuku* (worn originally by suicidal kamikaze bombers) and *sentofuku* (combat uniform). Riders typically wear *hachimaki* (headbands), sometimes with the rising sun or Imperial chrysanthemum crest at their centre, and groups carry flags announcing their names, which often evoke, without endorsing, nationalism. Some who wear the *sentofuku* even sport garishly painted hard hats, worn for show not for protection. The *sentofuku*, typically worn with lace-up boots, was originally the standard dress for right-wing groups and augments the *bosozoku* uniform's association with nationalist sentiment. But the groups are decidedly apolitical. Like the *Hakenkreuz* (the Nazi insignia) favoured by many Western bikers, decorations on these uniforms embody a set of social symbols that are either culturally discomforting or pleasingly nostalgic, depending on one's point of view. Groups scrawl their names – often in English – over the Imperial crest or rising sun, parodying the Japanese flag and co-opting nationalist images for their own self-styled collectives.

Ironically, the *bosozoku*'s militaristic, hypermasculine appearance is undercut by choices and practices that might be considered feminine. Rather than traditional black or dark blue, *tokkofuku* can be red, pink or white. Most *bosozoku* are beardless and sport carefully coiffed hair. This attention to self-presentation suggests if not a feminine fixation on personal appearance at least a decidedly unproletarian attachment to personal grooming. The evident expense involved in *tokkofuku* design and tailoring further sub-

Elaborately embroidered *bosozoku* costume.

Bosozoku in *tokkofuku* with club banner.

Bosozoku wearing *sentofuku* with helmets.

verts any real association with either the world of the military or that of the working class.

For the American club member, being a biker constitutes the totality of his identity. His devotion to his club is complete and unquestioned, and whether he is in the clubhouse or buying groceries, he is a club member. Being a *bosozoku*, however, is more event-driven: the costume, the motorcycle and the ride are all a piece of dramatic theatre, enacted as a public display to horrify/ amaze the public, and to identify the rider as *somebody*, as a *bosozoku*. The ride itself is a deliberate invocation of style. While speed is central to the *shinai boso*, acrobatic riding is crucial. Participants stress *medatsu* (being seen or looking conspicuous).[7] A risk-taker, a master of his machine, a fashion plate and a romantic adventurer/outlaw, the *bosozoku* acts as a character in a drama with a beginning (the gathering point), a middle (the thrilling ride) and an end (the post-ride decompression through conversation and boasting).

Bosozoku define themselves in two ways: as a member of a *bosozoku* club and as a *bosozoku* in contrast to a boring salaryman. In the past, relations between clubs were punctuated by violence, such as the June 1975 confrontation between the Tokyo Racing Club and Kanagawa Racing Club. However, like the events in Hollister, California, in July 1947 or the Mods–Rockers clashes of the 1964 Bank Holidays, one notable incident put the *bosozoku* squarely in the public consciousness. A public disturbance in 1976 in Kobe, attributed to the *bosozoku*, involved over 10,000 people, who burned vehicles, set fire to a police station and indirectly caused the death of a cameraman. For the media, and the public who consumed their stories, the *boso* tribes were a certified public menace.

Subsequent to these and other events, the *bosozoku* became, for the media and, by implication, the public, less of a descriptive term for youthful high speed urban racers and more of an appellation for an immoral public threat with potential ties to the Yakuza. Rather than a group of disaffected youths who broke the traffic laws, they became in the eyes of the media more generalized criminal gangs. The media thus enabled the public to conceptualize a shorthand for outsiders who posed a vague social threat: the *bosozoku*. In turn this demonization gave police agencies more latitude in the treatment of these alleged threats to overall social order. Once the vague threat to organized society is established in the public mind, sociologists, social psychologists, criminologists and others get in on the act, providing a rationale for this widespread deviance. It is only a few more steps until the vehicle of choice is made to stand for the supposed ethical defects of the rider: the motorcycle becomes a symbol of all that threatens the individual, the family, the social order and the future of the society.

Mods and Rockers

Like Japan, post-war Europe saw a rise in the visibility of teenagers as a social class, whose rising affluence, expanding leisure time and self-conscious alienation gave them a group identity, signalled by their preferred fashion: black leather jacket and jeans. A number of these groups gathered around motorcycles. In Sweden the press reported threats from the *Skinnknutte* (loosely translated as the 'leather lads'). The Germans and Austrians had the *Halb-starke* (or 'half-strong') and the French their *Blouson Noirs* ('Black Jackets').[8] In the lean times in early 1950s Britain, Teds and Leatherboys made their appearance. The Teds got their name from their stylized Edwardian dress: long velvet coats or waistcoats with stovepipe pants. Centred principally in London and a few provincial towns, the Teds parodied 'elegance', while the Leatherboys' outfits hearkened back to the threatening and romantic highwaymen. The Leatherboys also dominated motorcycle purchases in Britain. In the mid-1950s both Teds and Leatherboys, in their own way, were identified with delinquency.

With the rebirth of the British economy in the late 1950s and the rise of employment, British youth found themselves with jobs, money in their pockets and, on the weekend at least, precious leisure time. In class-sensitive Britain the public face of British youth seemed to manifest itself in two groups: office workers and manual or mechanical labourers. Drawing on earlier images of youth, these two groups became the most visible cultural icons linking youth and motorcycles: the Mods and the Rockers. A familiar pattern emerged: their iconic images also eventually embodied for the media the fear and fascination of deviance.

Office work appealed to those young people who were either children of the middle class or had middle-class aspirations. By the end of the 1950s Ted fashion was dying out, but the cultish self-display of the Teds coupled with their dandyish style no doubt gave these office workers ideas about their own sartorial choices, which centred on minor elements of clothing construction, such as vents, buttons, jacket length and shoe design.[9] The ostentatious display of the Teds, however, was muted. The focus was to be on neatness and cleanliness, an altogether 'Modern' look, inspired by Europe.[10] They wore slim Italian suits with short box jackets and narrow trousers in subdued colours, keeping their hair short in a carefully manicured 'French crew'. A green fishtail parka protected their outfits from the elements. In short, 'the mods invented a style which enabled them to negotiate smoothly between school, work and leisure, which concealed as much as it stated'.[11] Among themselves, however, they could pick out each other on the basis of stylistic details. Like the *bosozoku* they spent a lot of time hanging out, so

posture and stance were as important as clothing in embodying the 'look' of the Mod.

Given its relative inexpensiveness and promise of instant mobility, the scooter was an attractive transportation choice for a British youth in the late 1950s. For the Mods, the scooter – Lambretta or Vespa – was also neat, clean and stylishly European, the ideal choice for mobility, plus its step-through design and wide fairing provided protection for clothing and shoes. Mods' disposable income was spent not only on clothing, but on bike decoration. After Eddie Grimstead's 1959 decision to alter the look of the scooter with the addition of a flash paint job and, memorably, multiple mirrors or spotlights as decorative accessories, the scooter became an extension of individual fashion.[12] Like the *bosozoku*'s, the Mods' modifications had little, if anything, to do with performance and everything to do with style. Like the American club biker, the Mod saw his identity reflected in his modifications to his scooter. To the outsider, all chopped Harleys or mirror-encrusted scooters look pretty much the same, but as with the Mods' clothing it was the details that reflected the aesthetic and consumerist acumen of the scooter-proud Mod. His scooter, in fact, became the core of his existence. As a character in a recent novel explains, 'a Vespa was not merely a mode of transport but an ideology, family, friend and lover all rolled into one paragon of late 1940s engineering'.[13] He so prizes his green Vespa GS that he polishes it 'twice a day with a

Mods in a still from Franc Roddam's *Quadrophenia* (1979).
Rockers in a still from *Quadrophenia*.

baby's nappy' and encases it in a 'custom-built corrugated-iron shield'.[14]

The Mod, beset with boredom at his day job, wanted to squeeze every prized hour of fun he could from his weekend, gathering at the Flamingo or the Scene clubs, admiring others' scooters and dress, and listening to jazz-inspired blues, Motown sounds, Muddy Waters-inspired R&B or, eventually, West Indian ska and The Who.[15] As a result Mods turned to amphetamines to stay awake. The pills of choice, Drynamil, were nicknamed Purple Hearts or, sometimes, Blues.

Alongside Mod style developed another class-based movement, the Rockers. This group, focused more in rural areas than in London, emerged as an identifiable group in contrast to the Mods, descended not from the dandyish Teds but from the Leatherboys. Dressed in leather (often decorated with metal studs), denim and boots, with gravity-defying pompadour waves, the Rockers were working-class youths who broadcast toughness in their dress and demeanour, as well as their choice of transportation: motorcycles, not scooters. While as anxious as the Mods to demonstrate their aversion to conventional social values, they rejected the psycho-active drugs favoured by the Mods.

Unlike the Mods, the Rockers gave the appearance of 'true' bikers. They were devoted to the mechanical improvement of their bikes, unlike the cosmetic changes wrought on the Mods' scooters. The emphasis was on speed and the aerodynamic appearance of speed. The most memorable of these alterations was the Triton, a combination of a Triumph and a Norton. This bike, along with the café racers, such as the BSA Gold Star, Triumph Thunderbird and Velocette Venom, demonstrated the seriousness of the Rockers' com-mitment to developing a machine devoted to speed.

The Rockers had a favourite hangout, the Ace café, a truck stop on the North Circular Road. There and elsewhere – the Nightingale, the Busy Bee, the Salt Box – the Rockers met for drinks and racing, either from café to café (hence 'caff racing' and 'caff racers') or to reach the racing goal of 100 mph (a 'ton'). Like the *bosozoku* these young men were devoted to demonstrating their riding prowess on public roads, playing to an appreciative audience of girlfriends and mates and a fearful group of older citizens. As one Rocker described himself in 1964, 'I'm a Rocker because I ride a motorcycle. To be a Rocker, you've got to have a bike and a leather jacket with a studded belt, jeans and high topped racing boots. I wear my hair long by choice – with an elephant's trunk.'[16] Powerful machines, leather jackets, pompadours – these young men resembled the images they saw in US films such as *Blackboard Jungle* (1955) more than they did the leather-clad Hells Angels, whose look derived from American bomber pilots' wear from the Second World War.

While there was no love lost between the Mods and the Rockers, they can't be said to have been enemies. However, two 1964 Bank Holiday confrontations, one in Clacton over the Easter weekend, the other in Brighton, Margate and Hastings over the Whitsun holiday (the Brighton episode memorably reenacted in the 1979 film *Quadrophenia*), gave both media and citizens an opportunity to crystallize their fear over this newly empowered class of young people as 'gangs' prone to rioting, vandalism and generalized public disturbance. Just as there were conflicts in Hollister, California, in 1947, there were clashes between groups of youths identifiable as Mods and Rockers. However, owing to the need of the media to attract consumers, these events were presented as much more dramatic and violent than they actually were. Headlines read 'The Bank Holiday Offenders'[17] or 'The Mods and Rockers invade'.[18] The overreaction of the judiciary and other local officials gave the public further reason for fright and the young people further reason for alienation and resentment. Fines were issued out of all proportion to the mostly petty offences, creating economic hardships for these poorly paid office workers and labourers.[19] These isolated events, as for the *bosozoku*, gave the media the opportunity to demonize groups of young people. Following the Whitsun holiday skirmishes papers quoted a magistrate in Margate, who called them 'long-haired, unkempt, mentally unstable, petty little saw-dust caesars [who] could only find courage by hunting like rats in packs'.[20] Another magistrate in Hastings described the ruckus in his town as an 'invasion of adolescent morons'.[21] Rather than focusing on the specific acts of vandalism or violence, the media created an association in the mind of the public of Mods and Rockers as somehow synonymous with moral defectiveness and a 'national problem'. By creating a class of relatively powerless 'deviants', the newspaper-reading public could give a name to their fears and feel a surge of self-satisfaction that they weren't part of that 'lot'.

Hells Angels

In the popular mind in the US, one type of motorcycle club is paramount, the 'patch' club. Originating in the US following the Second World War (and subsequently expanding worldwide), these clubs were comprised of young returning war veterans. Single, largely uneducated, disaffected from the social expectations of reintegration into the world of jobs and families, these men sought a sense of identity and belonging, and nowhere did they find those elements more strongly than among their club members. As Chuck Zito says, 'We wanted to be like the gangs depicted in movies – tough sons of bitches who didn't like authority and weren't afraid of anyone, guys who looked out for one another and fought for one another.'[22] Sporting colourful names such as the Booze Fighters, the clubs' social activities revolved around working on bikes, riding bikes and drinking, punctuated by the occasional high spirited brawl.[23]

As clubs proliferated and evolved, so did their internal organization. Official positions within the club were established and members were elected. Principal officers consisted of a president, a vice-president, a treasurer, a sergeant-at-arms (the latter to enforce order) and, in the case of group rides, a ride captain, whose job it was to ensure the club's safety, order and protection while on the road.

Clubs also produced a constitution or set of rules governing the club's structure and expectations for members' conduct. For example, members must ride a certain kind of motorcycle (a Harley-Davidson), pay dues, attend a certain number of meetings per year, participate in club activities and so forth. Punishments were outlined for members who failed to follow the rules. Rules for becoming a member included an explicit probationary period for prospective members ('prospects'), duties while a prospect (usually involving some onerous task, such as sweeping out the clubhouse regularly) and voting requirements for successful admission (prospects could be 'blackballed' by one or more negative votes). By becoming part of the group, it was assumed that the club was the central focus of a member's life. A musketeer-like sense of brotherhood developed, exemplified in the assumption that an attack on one was an attack on all. As Hunter Thompson notes, 'Despite the anarchic possibilities of the machines they ride and worship, [Hells Angels] insist that their main concern in life is "to be a righteous Angel," which requires a loud obedience to the party line.'[24]

The notion of a rigid, organized hierarchy, explicit rules and punishment for violators, and elaborate requirements for prospective members all evoke the military past of most of the members. The military not only formed the characters of these relatively uneducated young men, but also gave them a template for establishing post-war social relations with one another, in which they saw in the group an active justification for rejecting the bourgeois social expectations they encountered on return to civilian life.

These clubs were established along geographic lines and, early on, political negotiations, augmented by occasional violent conflict, established the 'turf' of each club. Like the rigid rules governing the club internally, uncompromising expectations were established about the geographic scope of the club and its rights to the name of the club. Groups of motorcyclists in another geographic area who wished to form a club needed sanction from either presidents of the other clubs, or the president of the founding club. Sanctioning a new chapter often included a visit to the proposed club's city by the president or his representative, an informal but explicit vetting process of the members of the proposed new chapter and assurances of their willingness to abide by the club's established rules.

From the mid-1950s and the decades that followed, four major patch clubs were established in North America and elsewhere: the Hells Angels, the Bandidos, the Pagans and the Outlaws. Collectively, these are known as 'outlaw' motorcycle clubs. (Ironically, the term 'outlaw' did not originally derive from the clubs' alleged illegal activities, but from the choice of some individuals to participate in non-American Motorcycle Association (AMA)-sanctioned racing events or 'outlaw' races.)[25] The Hells Angels (sometimes called the 'Big Red Machine') consists of more than 200 chapters in 13 states in the USA, and over 200 international chapters in 25 countries, with a global membership estimated to be between 2,000 and 3,000. As Sonny Barger, famed president of the Hells Angels Oakland Chapter, says, 'The sun never sets on a Hell's Angel patch'.[26] The Bandidos membership rivals the Hells Angels' internationally, with over 2,500 members – 1,000 in 81 chapters in 15 states, and 1,500 in 12 other countries. By contrast,

the Outlaws have 63 chapters in 16 states, and 8 international chapters, while the Pagans have only 44, all in the US.[27]

Becoming a member of one of these clubs entitles the participant to wear the club's 'patch', usually a set of three insignias sewn onto the back of a sleeveless denim jacket. The top semi-circular patch or 'rocker' displays the club's name, mirrored on the bottom by a patch bearing the name of the city where the club is located. In the

Vietnam veterans' motorcycle club patch.

middle is an emblem representing the club, often employing traditionally aggressive images, such as death's heads, swords or knives. The patch, along with the member's bike, is his most important possession and any attempt to deprive the wearer of his patch is expected to be met with aggressive hostility. Members who disgrace the club in any way are required to return the patch to the club, and any other symbols of belonging, such as tattoos, are obliterated. The analogy with symbols of military rank and their removal subsequent to a soldier disgracing the military is obvious.

This phenomenon is made even more curious by the other associations, originally peculiar to US cyclists, that have been adopted worldwide. One potent analogy for the motorcyclist is the equation of the motorcycle with the horse, his 'iron steed'. Like the *bosozoku*'s association with the samurai, this image hearkens back to two powerful images: the European medieval knight and his more modern US counterpart, the Western hero. The latter, the solitary, taciturn, dusty but beautifully attired master of the horse and the six-gun, engenders what might be called a double nostalgia. On the one hand, the motorcyclist can look backward to a time when independent men could define themselves through the measured but ever-present possibility of violence. Correlatively, he can look forward, to the opportunity to demonstrate his social independence and singular values alongside a band of like-minded brothers. The motorcyclist can enact his indifference to the commercial values of contemporary bourgeois society by mounting his iron steed and riding out into the trackless waste of the interstate highway system.

Such an image has an obvious appeal to working-class men in particular, who often feel hemmed in by the oppressive obligations of getting by, especially in a society that undervalues their mechanical skills, denies them a decent salary or opportunities for professional advancement. No wonder, then, that the chance to mount a motorcycle and, at highway speeds, act out an exciting, honourable mythic narrative exerts such a powerful appeal, not only to Americans but to riders everywhere. In Germany, for example, the novels of Karl May (1842–1912), featuring Old Shatterhand and his Indian friend, Winnetou, demonstrate what a powerful international figure the Western hero can be. For the non-American, to own or ride a Harley-Davidson motorcycle allows the rider, through his consumption of the motorcycle, to participate in the grand romantic US tradition of playing the cowboy.

It should be clear, however, that equating the motorcyclist with the Western hero involves the fuzziest of associations. The Western hero sought, through his mediation between the 'civilized' settlers and the 'barbaric' forces of the wilderness (Indians or gunslingers), to avoid violence, using it only as a last resort in the iconic final gun battle. For the club member, however, violence is a means of self-definition, a response to what he sees as a hostile and alien environment. The Western hero's attitude toward women, like that of the knight before him, was chivalric – they needed respect and protection. Today his attitude may be understood as benign social repression, but within the context of the Western hero's worldview he treated women properly. While it is impossible to generalize about patch club members' attitudes toward women – some Hells Angels chapters had women as members during the 1950s – we can generally say that women are subordinates, if not functioning servants, in these clubs.

On the other side of the civilization–wilderness divide of the Western we can observe another powerful image for the club member: the Indian band of brothers. Proud, independent, resource-ful, the Indian band of riders defended themselves from threats from without, not only from the encroaching settlers, but also bands of Indian warriors from other tribes. This image of unity-until-death in a hostile environment is a powerful one for the club, and gives the member a way of understanding his group and his role in it.

Again, just as with the analogy of the Western hero, this image of the band of brothers is serviceable so long as one doesn't look too closely. While it may be true that both groups suffer from social repression and undeserved violence from forces purporting to be the law of the land, their 'independence' from the society around them has clear and different roots. The patch club member's independence stems largely from a sense of social alienation, a rejection of bourgeois values and a willingness to live on what he sees as the fringes of society (imaginatively, that divide between civilization and wilderness). The Indians, of course, were genuinely independent of the Anglo social and economic order, and surrendered their independence only when faced with the barrel of a gun.

However nebulously understood, the motorcycle patch club, emerging as it has from a confluence of technology and social conditions, has developed into a powerful international image of social rebellion and self-definition. Of course, the young Lithuanian man, tearing around Vilnius on his Harley, sporting his tattoos, shades and hostile expression, has never been to America or met a Hells Angel in his life. What he has done is gone to the movies.

On the weekend of America's Independence Day celebration, 4 July 1947, a number of motorcyclists rode into the town of Hollister, California (population 4,500), an agricultural community, to drink, ride their bikes and roughhouse. Hollister had hosted AMA races in the 1930s. The Second World War had interrupted the races, but 'Hollister' still had resonance for motorcyclists. Accounts differ on the number of riders – from a few hundred to four thousand – but there were too many cyclists for the town's tiny, seven-man police force.

Gathering on San Benito Street – the main drag – fuelled by beer from the town's many bars, cyclists staged races and games (relay races, wheelies, etc.), while mostly ignoring the races being conducted at nearby Memorial Park. By Sunday, approximately 50–60 bikers had been injured, and an equal number arrested. The California Highway patrol arrived that afternoon, and the bikers dispersed homeward.

The San Francisco Chronicle and other papers sensationalized the event through their headlines, but most damaging and influential was the clearly staged photograph in the 21 July issue of *Life* magazine of a drunken lout astride a motorcycle surrounded by broken beer bottles. The photograph, 'Cyclist's Holiday', was taken for, but never published in, the *San Francisco Chronicle*.[28] It was picked up by *Life*, where the image of the drunken biker appeared opposite another photograph titled 'Barber's Holiday', which showed a mannequin in an ape mask in a barber's chair. The obvious implication was that bikers were simian creatures who engaged in loutish, animalistic behaviour – instinct run wild. 'He and friends terrorize a town', read the caption. Less obvious was that the photo of the cyclist was as clearly composed as the photo of the mannequin. While accounts differ, the rotund drunkard may not have been among the bikers but a local conscripted to pose.[29] All agree, however, that photographer Barney Peterson staged the scene, piling bottles around and under the bike's wheels for effect. No rider would have deliberately parked on broken glass.

Harper's Magazine subsequently published Frank Rooney's short story, 'The Cyclists' Raid', and Hollywood producer Stanley Kramer acquired the screen rights to the story for *The Wild One*. Directed by Lásló Benedek, starring Marlon Brando and Lee Marvin, the film opened in February 1954 to respectable but not spectacular business. While *The Wild One* may not have originally been much as a business

BARBER'S HOLIDAY

He departs and leaves ape behind

CYCLIST'S HOLIDAY

He and friends terrorize a town

proposition, as a popular culture document it is ground-breaking and historically significant, instantly creating a set of unforgettable images: of the motorcycle 'gang' as it breaks the crest of a hill during the electrifying opening, of the motorcycle 'tough' Chino (Lee Marvin), who lives only to ride his bike and brawl and, of course, the misunderstood, taciturn, beautiful, rebellious youth, Johnny Strabler.

From François Villon to Byron to Jean Genet, the outlaw as anti-hero has functioned as a common social trope. So Marlon Brando's portrayal of Johnny Strabler as the leader of a motorcycle gang called the Black Rebels, who terrorized the sleepy movie town of Wrightsville with his buddies, should come as no surprise. Nor should the fact that, in his black leather jacket and blue jeans, he was deemed worthy of both sartorial and behavioural imitation. What is surprising is the scope and influence of this image. Motorcyclists from around the world took Johnny and Chino as types worthy of emulation. (Given that Brando's character eclipsed

'Barber's Holiday', *Life*, 21 July 1947.

'Cyclist's Holiday', *Life*, 21 July 1947.

that of Marvin's as a pop cultural icon, it's interesting that Marvin rode a Harley-Davidson Flathead, while Brando rode a 650cc Triumph Thunderbird.) But the image didn't move only in one direction, from pop culture icon to consumer. Just as Mafia members took cues on dress and comportment from *The Godfather*, the President of the Hells Angels San Francisco chapter, Frank Sadilek,

Chino (Lee Marvin) rides into town in Laszlo Bénédek's *The Wild One* (1954).

Johnny Strabler (Marlon Brando) gets tough with Kathie Bleeker (Mary Murphy) in *The Wild One*.

bought and wore the blue-and-yellow striped T-shirt sported by Lee Marvin's character in the film.[30]

Clad in leather and denim, Brando (along with his contemporary James Dean) embodied youthful alienation. It was an image after which motorcyclists could fashion themselves. Tough and rebellious, misunderstood and sensitive, Johnny, not Chino, became the man who represented all that was simultaneously seductive and repellent about the motorcyclist, an 'outlaw' women (supposedly) found irresistible.

As we have seen in Japan and Britain, the press in effect transformed the biker into a deviant. The sensational *Life* magazine photo taken at Hollister spawned a raft of press coverage of these hard-drinking, hard-partying threats to social order. And again we can see that it is a short step from the identification of the social deviant to the symbolization of deviance by its mechanical media fetish object, the motorcycle.

The paradox of identity

In all three of these cases we can consider motorcycle clubs and all the external markers of solidarity (dress, hairstyle, choice of motorcycle, music, etc.) as efforts to resist mainstream culture and create a self-definition unconstrained by conventional expectations. Joining a group is paradoxical in that the biker's identity disappears into that of the group, but out of this submersion arises a liberating sense of individuality. It should come as no surprise that all three examples involve predominately male youth and a purportedly 'dangerous' machine, given the adolescent's natural process of identity formation and naïve sense of immortality.

Yet one might ask why, in the inevitable process of self-definition that is maturation, do young people need to congregate in groups? A key to the appeal of the clubs is some lack on the part of the individual: money, education or other forms of social power. Young people are in a transitional phase between their dependence on their parents and their independence as adults, and this transition can be eased by the reinforcement that belonging to a group brings, and the anxiety-born requirements of dress, language and behaviour exacted by the group, what Dick Hebdige calls 'a celebration of impotence'.[31]

Perhaps more interesting than youths who gather in groups and in their various cultural ways transgress boundaries is the social reaction to these (often minor) transgressions. The ascription of 'deviance' to certain kinds of social behaviour, despite its heavy moral weight in media accounts, is a description, not a judgement. Motorcycle club members are different in various ways from the dominant culture, but that doesn't make them bad. Consider the

Russian teenagers on motorcycles, 1990.

Mods' drug taking: media accounts portray ingesting methamphetamines as somehow morally suspect, while reporting to a public awash in alcohol and nicotine. The elaborate silliness of the *bosozoku* costumes in no way resembles the seriousness of the salaryman's suit, but both serve to conceal the person's nakedness and protect them from inclement weather. An assumption of deviance stems from the dominant culture's possession of power, not right. The elaborate dance between the dominant culture and its 'deviant' members should be understood as an objective relation, not a clash between the morally upright and the morally defective.

As Stanley Cohen has noted, 'deviance doesn't lead to social control; social control leads to deviance'.[32] Collectors of Hummel figurines are not considered deviant because their practices aren't particularly interesting and do not seem to embody values different from the dominant culture. However, groups that seem to enact values that challenge those of the dominant culture are, by definition, deviant. And when those challengers are either attractive, owing to their youthfulness, or seemingly menacing, owing to their aggressive dress and loud bikes, they become focal points for media attention.

The dominant culture will generally attempt to use some sort of force against the deviants to forestall or control their behaviour or

Motorcycle club out to enjoy autumn colours along the Mohawk Trail, Massachusetts, October 1941.

dress, usually the police. This attempt attracts media attention, and the media then take the opportunity to define the group as a group ('rioters', 'gangs', 'addicts' and so forth). While most groups that gather around a focal object, such as a motorcycle, are quite varied in their values and goals, media attention rigidifies the meaning of the group identity. For example, people who like to ride motorcycles in groups become 'bikers', with all the cultural accretions that have grown around that term.[33] Force and external media definition further isolate the club from the dominant culture and, at a certain point, the group itself, in trying to define itself, declares others do not belong to the group: an orthodontist riding his Harley on the weekend is not a 'real biker'. Signs of group identity then become more fraught as the pressure for internal definition increases. One of the more interesting examples of this occurs in *Quadrophenia*, when Jimmy is having a public bath and finds himself in a singing 'contest' with the young man in the adjacent stall. Hearing snatches of Gene Vincent's lyrics 'Bebop a lula / She's my baby', sung by his neighbouring bather, Jimmy asks – at first politely – that he stop with that 'old rubbish'. Naturally, this makes the offended Rocker only sing louder, inciting Jimmy to counter with strains of 'You Really Got Me' by the Kinks.

Jimmy emerges from his tub and looks over the wall at his neighbour and recognizes a former school chum, Kev. Only later, when they meet up at a café, does Jimmy realize that, while he is a Mod, Kev is a Rocker, with his leather attire and pompadour.

Jimmy: 'Ere, I never realized.
Kev: Never realized what?
Jimmy: You's a rocker.
Kev: What, am I black or something?
Jimmy: Well you ain't exactly white in that sort of get up, are you?

Part of the subsequent dramatic conflict is Jimmy's desire to renew his friendship with his chum and the social pressure exacted by the other Mods to prevent Jimmy from doing so.

Once the deviant group has been identified, symbolic transfer can occur with the group's marks of identity. The motorcycle becomes identified as 'dangerous' and those who ride it 'outlaws'. In capitalist cultures, the image becomes commodified and market-ed. The ubiquity of Harley-Davidson products, from coffee mugs to living room rugs, is a case in point. As the images of deviancy are sold to the public in concrete form, the 'deviants' reject those images, seeking out more extreme forms of display and behaviour (for example, the Hells Angels' alleged practice of soaking their colours in motor oil, creating occasions to provoke club-on-club violence, etc.). As the deviance becomes more extreme, it becomes

Advertisement for Harley-Davidson products, *Holiday Gift Guide* 2004.

a self-fulfilling prophecy for the dominant culture, and the deviants' behaviour becomes a 'growing social plague' that threatens some delicate and attractive part of the culture, such as children or teenage girls. Injustices perpetrated against the deviant group (such as the outrageously large fines given following the Mods–Rockers confrontation in Brighton) seem justified, as if the choice to be a Mod was a totally autonomous act.

Over time, the increased pressure to conform to group expectations can drive away some of its members. Changes occur in individual members' lives that cause them to drift away (they graduate from school, get another job, etc.). In the case of the *bosozoku*, members are expected to leave the group as they age, and expected to transition from motorcycles to cars as soon as they are old enough. Because fashion is by definition constantly changing, group members may feel 'outdated' in their identification with the group. Eventually, only those who for various reasons cannot integrate themselves into the dominant culture remain.

As a result, some groups have deliberately defined themselves in reaction against the prevailing negative image of the biker as 'outlaw'. If the biker subculture has been defined as predominantly white, male and heterosexual, then women and gays, as well as riders from racial and ethnic minorities, have to fight for visibility among motorcyclists and in the media.

The Motor Maids

The persistent popular association of motorcyclists and motorcycling with men has meant that women, in particular, have appeared as oddities. In part, this stems from perceptions of the vehicle itself as a mechanical device designed for speed. Motorcycles originated at the turn of the twentieth century, coinciding with the publication of a host of scientific 'studies' confirming women's fragility. These studies emerged owing to the popularization of Darwin's theory of natural selection, which held that sex differences resulted from evolution. Social Darwinists appropriated evolutionary theory to argue that such differences are decisive and 'natural', and that any violations threatened the very survival of the species. Such arguments, of course, obviously partake of the naturalistic fallacy, claiming that we have moral obligations based on certain facts of existence. They make the mistake of trying to derive *prescriptive* statements from *descriptive* ones. In addition, they are essentialist, arguing that innate biological differences between males and females determine social behaviour and cultural differences between men and women.

Despite their obvious logical flaws, arguments circulated against, for instance, providing women with an education on the grounds that it would damage their reproductive capacities. Such assumptions rested on the belief that women had a lesser amount of energy or 'life force' than men, presumed to be carried by bodily fluids such as blood. Her obligation was to channel her energies into reproduction. Women who diverted their energy – intellectual or physical – would become weak, nervous, sterile or bear neurotic children. Reading would, according to the scientists, make women's uteruses shrink.[34] The same specious logic was used to bar women from any pursuit that might divert their energies or potentially damage their reproductive organs, including riding a motorcycle.

From a technological standpoint, no necessary link exists between man and machine. Early riders of motorized bicycles at the end of the nineteenth century included both men and women, bicycling being a popularly accepted pastime for both sexes. A 1904 item in *The Motor Cycle* reports on women racers in France: 'the two rivals are most daring drivers, and take the corners without the slightest hesitation, and with every confidence'.[35] They were expected to be not only fast but capable with a wrench. A report published the next month on a 100-mile ride by Mary E. Kennard opined, 'The heart knoweth its own bitterness, and no motorcyclist is free from trouble. Sex does not secure exemption, and the wise woman learns how to help herself out of an ordinary difficulty.'[36]

Adverts for motorcycle manufacturers worldwide in the 1910s and '20s featured women. *Motor Cycle Illustrated*, for example, ran an ad in its 22 February 1917 issue for Excelsior, boasting about its ease of maintenance and featuring a female model. The British motorcycle industry specifically attempted to target women to increase its overall sales in the 1920s. Like bicycle manufacturers they featured female riders in print advertisements and posters.[37] The motorcycle press joined the campaign by appointing women to write articles for a female readership. Mabel Lockwood-Tatham, for example, wrote a column called 'Through Feminine Goggles' for *The Motor Cycle*. The 'Entirely for Eve' column in *Motor Cyclist Review* was written by 'Cylinda' (a Latinate play on cylinder?). They offered practical advice, including information about motorcycle maintenance.

At the same time female riders appealed to the non-riding public in the popular press. Marjorie Cottle, a leading sports rider and probably Britain's best-known female motorcyclist, confided in an article which appeared in the *Evening Standard*:

Once, not so very long ago, the woman motor-cyclist was regarded as something of a crank or a freak. Times have changed, and motor-cycling as a sport is becoming more and more popular with women. It has been conclusively proved that motor-cycling is not harmful to women.[38]

February 22, 1917.   Motor Cycle Illustrated   1

Here Is a Time Saver

No matter how good the Motorcycle, or how careful the user, carbon will accumulate; its entire removal necessitating removing and scraping the cylinders.

Ordinarily, this means tearing down the whole Motorcycle.

In the Series 18 Excelsior, simply detach the gasoline and oil pipes, remove the two bolts at the ends of the center bar. Then swing the center bar and gasoline tank to the side, giving perfect access to the cylinders and pistons, without removing the motorcycle from the frame, or interference with any other part of the machine.

It changes a day's job to a matter of minutes. If you do the work yourself it saves hours of time. If it is done by the repairman it saves dollars in money.

It is one of the big points of Excelsior supremacy, appreciated mainly by the man who has been through the mill.

It is another reason why you should ride an Excelsior.

EXCELSIOR MOTOR MFG. & SUPPLY CO.
Office and Factory, 3703 Cortland St., Chicago

Instead, she, like other women riders of the time, argued the opposite: motorcycling was a healthy activity. She said, 'Girls will find that motor-cycling brings health. It will give them honest, fresh-air complexions. It will make them hardy and strong.' Twin sisters Betty and Nancy Debenham, both ardent motorcycle enthusiasts, wrote that 'motor-cycling is an ideal hobby for the tired business girl. She can seek health and pleasure during her precious weekends by exploring the countryside and the seaside.'[39]

Early female enthusiasts defended themselves against charges that the sport made them 'mannish', declaring that the woman motorcyclist was still appropriately feminine. Cottle added that

Excelsior advertisement featuring a female mechanic, *Motor Cycle Illustrated*, 22 February 1917.

'although the powder puff is not a part of the girl motor-cyclist's make-up it can always be hidden away for use when occasion demands it'. The Debenham sisters envisioned female riders gathering 'violets and primroses from the woods'.

Arguments with perhaps more basis in fact cited women's lack of strength in comparison to men. Women, it was claimed, were not physically able to operate the heavy machinery of the motorcycle. The Debenham sisters, however, assured women that while the motorcycle used to be 'something for young giants to urge into pulsating life . . . [T]oday there are wonderful little machines which start with the very first kick and with most precocious appetites for roadfaring.' In fact, British designers crafted lightweight models specifically for women. A reporter from *The Daily Mirror*, who had attended the 1921 Motor Cycle Show in London, enthused that he had seen 'the daintiest and prettiest little vehicles imaginable. . . perfectly adapted for shopping excursions as for long runs in the country and to the sea'.[40]

Such efforts resulted in failure – for both the British motorcycle industry and women. Instead, dubious arguments offered with seemingly unimpeachable bases in biology and biomechanics, as well as persistent associations of technology and speed with masculinity, undercut attempts to enhance and facilitate women's participation in motorcycling and undermined these early attempts to create a community of female riders. In the US female riders were still perceived as oddities. Sisters Augusta and Adeline Van Buren rode cross-country on individual motorcycles in 1916, determined to demonstrate that women could ride as dispatch couriers for the war effort and thus remove one argument used to deny women the vote: the fact that women did not participate in war.[41]

Rather than part of a like-minded collective, female pioneers of the 1920s and '30s saw themselves as individuals and asserted

tional 1940s housewife image by wearing pink outfits, keeping herself consistently manicured and coiffed (she even attached a lipstick holder to her motorcycle), and having each of her many (over 35) motorcycles painted pink. She said, 'I've made people realize that not all of us are like the bearded, black-leather-jacketed hoods that the media tars us with.'[47] While the club did require that members legally own and operate their own motorcycle or one belonging to a family member, female riders – in dress and self-presentation – went to great pains to identify themselves as feminine, as their name, 'maids', suggests. Their uniform adapted the more masculine attire donned for racing and military service: silver-gray slacks, royal blue over-blouse with white boots and tie. Participating in their first parade in 1941, the Motor Maids added white gloves, an established

Military uniforms, yes, but respectably feminine. Three generations of Motor Maid riders, c. 1948: Dot Robinson with her mother riding pillion, accompanied by Dot's daughter, Betty Fauls.

marker of mannered femininity, to their uniform and became known as the 'Ladies of the White Gloves'.[48]

The slogans of the many clubs founded on this original model stress 'mutual support' and 'recognition', while promoting 'a positive image of motorcycling'. By this they mean resistance at once to the association of motorcycle clubs with outlaws and to conceptions of the female rider as inappropriately masculine. To this day the Motor Maids claim, 'We believe that presenting a positive image of women motorcyclists demonstrates our RESPECT for each other and for ourselves.'[49] Their conception of 'respect' differs markedly from that of male riders. American Chuck Zito, for instance, claims in his autobiography, *Street Justice*, that 'it's about respect'.[50] In his case, having others respect him is not something he desires, but a response he demands. He says, 'when it comes to the issue of respect, I am utterly without flexibility'.[51] When he does not get it, he resorts to violence. By contrast, the Motor Maids are seeking, not demanding, respect. Rather than through violence, they show their respect through their self-presentation, in solidarity with each other and to the eyes of a judging public. While in both cases the perceived need for respect belies a sense of anxiety and inadequacy, the female motorcycle club members are willing to change themselves to get it rather than force others to give it.

Along traditionally feminine lines, they do so through self-presentation and self-fashioning. The Motor Maids cite Dot for uniting women riders and showing 'that you could ride a motorcycle and still be a lady'. They tell their favourite story, from a Honda dealer in Sarasota, Florida, who 'chased that woman for two days, through mud and trees' but never caught her. At the end of the race, while the men hit the local bar, Dot returned to her room to clean up, eventually appearing in the bar 'in a black sheath dress and a pill box hat'. The lesson for the Motor Maids?

'Dot was always a lady. . . She proved that you can be a lady, still compete with the men and not be a man-hater.'[52] Even in the new millennium, contemporary members are at pains to define themselves as appropriately feminine.

While they do not say so explicitly, the Motor Maids' reference to 'man-haters' signals their anxiety about being labelled as inadequately female, as 'mannish' or lesbian. While some lesbian riders have embraced the moniker of 'Dykes on Bikes',[53] other women's groups with homosexual affiliations appear interested in distancing themselves from the label. The Sirens Motorcycle Club of New York City describes itself simply as one of 'the country's leading women's motorcycle clubs'. The rainbow flag on their website suggests at the very least their endorsement and support of alternative sexualities, as does the fact that they 'are proud to organize and lead the motorcycle contingent for New York City's Lesbian, Gay, Bisexual, Transgender Pride March'.[54]

The majority of contemporary women's motorcycle clubs seek neither to establish their members as equals of male riders nor to reject debilitating, stereotypical definitions of female riders as inadequately feminine. Instead, they define themselves as distinctly women-identified collectives, championing values directly opposed to those typically associated with men, especially individualism and competition, repeatedly citing qualities such as sisterhood and support, caring and cooperation.

Women on Wheels, founded in 1982 in California, promises to 'unite all women motorcycle enthusiasts for recreation, education, mutual support, recognition, and to promote a positive image of motorcycling'. The similarly named Women in the Wind claims to 'unite women motorcyclists with friends of common interest, and promote a positive image to the public of women on motorcycles'. Again, with chapters named Steel Magnolias, Diamond Roses and

Riding Divas, by 'positive image' they appear to mean 'feminine'. Leather & Lace have built, in their words, a 'strong sisterhood' of 'independent women who share a common bond of riding'. Even though the club's name suggests a blurring of masculinity and femininity, their rhetoric clearly stresses the frilly femininity of 'lace' more than leather. The proliferation of motorcycle clubs using the term 'lady' suggests the persistence of efforts to define women riders as feminine: Ladies' Bike Club, Ladies in the Wind, Lady Cycle Riders, Lady Lucifers, etc.

Some organizations do seem less anxious about the image of the female motorcyclist. WIMA, the Women's International Motorcycle

The start of a motorcycle race at a police show.

Association, was founded in the 1950s and is now the largest women's international motorcycle organization. Its founder, Louise Scherbyn, had been a member of the Motor Maids but dismissed them as more a display team than a motorcycle club. Instead, she corresponded with women from other countries and became convinced there should be 'a world wide organisation for all women motorcyclists'.[55] Nonetheless, the organization embraces typically 'feminine' values. The British chapter defends WIMA as a club just for women on the basis that it offers 'a uniquely non-competitive, supportive and encouraging atmosphere'.[56]

A secondary purpose of all such clubs is to contribute to the general community, not simply the community of women riders. Male motorcycle clubs have also attempted to resist cultural definitions of riding as 'outlaw' behaviour by engaging in charitable work, such as organizing toy runs for underprivileged children at Christmas or riding the Trail of Tears to commemorate displaced Native Americans. Women's groups, however, define their community engagement along gendered lines, promoting their work as women on behalf of other women or children. In WIMA's words, they are dedicated 'to mak[ing] the world a better place for women by supporting worthy charities'. The Nubian Nation, an all-female group of African-American riders, describes itself as active in community affairs.[57] Many groups, including the Sirens and Spokes-Women, cite their participation in rides dedicated to raising money for the Susan G. Komen Breast Cancer Foundation. And several raise money for women's crisis services or organizations supporting victims of domestic violence. Others, endorsing the essentialist view of women as caring nurturers, owing to their ability to reproduce, highlight their commitments to children as well. By continuing to define themselves in opposition to male groups and the majority of male riders, however, women's groups

– perhaps unwittingly – persist in upholding stereotypes even when they claim to resist them.

Women's response to their perceived social position as riders provides some interesting analogies with the male club members. The 'deviant' label attached to young male motorcyclists by the media and other groups – whatever the country – demonstrated not the deviance of the cyclists, but the power of those who controlled the media, judiciary and other social institutions to name and control the behaviour of groups that didn't conform to bourgeois social expectations. Analogously, women find themselves in the same structural position in a male-oriented society. In the same way that *bosozoku*, Mods and Rockers, and 'outlaw' motorcyclists defined themselves and promoted their values on the basis of their opposition to the dominant social groups, women's motorcycle clubs find themselves in the same position of relative powerlessness, prompting them to define themselves in opposition to the values of the male motorcyclists and motorcycle clubs, a condition that in other circumstances has been called 'internal colonialism'. Hence, the women are bikers, but still 'feminine', and dedicated not to brawling, but to making the world a better place. While there is obviously nothing wrong with women extolling feminine values, it is unfortunate that the motivating force appears to be anxiety about one's social identity.

A solution to such problems of self-definition and understanding of the female motorcycle community may lie not in riders but in the motorcycle itself. Changes in motorcycle design and demographics have challenged cultural perceptions of bikers that have negatively affected female riders. The motorcycle of choice for members of the stereotyped 'outlaw' clubs has been the cruiser, particularly the Harley-Davidson brand. Yet, all the while, the Harley-Davidson Sportster, owing to its relative compactness and low seat height, has been the bike of choice for many women motorcyclists, challenging

the masculinist image of Harley-Davidson. Innovations in light-weight metal alloys (such as carbon fibre) and engine design have created an increasing range of commercially available motorcycles that are even lighter and more manoeuvrable. In short, nothing in the design of contemporary motorcycles disadvantages women owing to their lesser strength or stature in comparison to men. In addition, younger riders have increasingly turned to sportbikes, which, owing to both aesthetics and purpose, carry different associations than heavyweight cruisers.

Designed for speed, sportbikes participate in the culture of racing that has dominated in Britain and Europe. The original British clubs established at the turn of the twentieth century emphasized the sporting side, providing rules and guidelines for conducting trials,

Racer Rhiannon Lucente.

races and other forms of competition. They attracted enthusiasts interested in testing their skills from all classes and both sexes.[58]

Adapted from motorcycles raced on tracks, sportbikes appeal to riders of both sexes interested in testing their limits individually and in competition. The sportbiker's riding gear is also derived from the track: riders typically wear adaptations of racing leathers and full helmets, muting the gender differences typically on display among riders of other motorcycles. On the track, all riders appear androgynous, the rider fused with the machine. That bike disappearing around the curve could be piloted by a man or a woman.

Still, sportbikes tend to sustain the associations of motorcycling with men. Its high speeds associate motorcycling with risk and danger, typically configured as masculine. Popular representations of sportbike culture, such as *Biker Boyz* and *Torque*, feature few female riders and perpetuate images of scantily clad females as mere accessories. Contemporary media accounts of sportbike riders weaving aggressively in and out of traffic or recklessly performing wheelies on the highway perpetuate the image of the 'outlaw' biker intent on menacing the local citizenry.

Closing the circle

Owing to the association of motorcycles with social deviance, a complex and reciprocally reinforcing dance occurs between a club member and the larger culture. Not only does the biker define who he is, the society defines what he is not by declaring the biker deviant. Exactly how this deviance expresses itself is a function of the culture in which the biker finds himself. What can be said is that, while there can be many different ways groups can congregate around a motorcycle, the clubs that attract media attention and hence engender a number of socially symbolic associations are those with young men as their members. In post-war Japan and Britain young people became newly empowered with an economic clout unknown during their parents' youth. Combine the young's tendency toward self-definition through negation of accepted social models with youthful affluence and one has the extraordinary costumes of the *bosozoku* and the Mods. Supply urban youth with limited funds and transportation choices and they will naturally happen on a vehicle that is inexpensive to run and capable of being modified to exhibit one's individuality: the motorcycle. News organizations and purveyors of fictional narratives label these trends 'deviant', producing the expected (and lucrative) public outrage, adoption of the often cartoonlike image of 'deviance' by a larger cross section of the young, and commodification of the image by those who produce and sell products, such as clothing manufacturers and movie studios. The young consume the movies, further modifying their look and behaviour to reflect the alluring screen images, and the circle is closed. After a period in which each group profits in its own way, boredom and the need for novelty, alongside aging of the young and changing social conditions, produce new images. Increasingly motorcycling is becoming identified with the affluent in the West (i.e. RUBs, Rich Urban Bikers, a phenomenon Suzanne McDonald-Walker calls 'a gentrification of rebellion').[59] Since this identification better reflects the demographic information about contemporary riders, the cultural association between motorcycling and deviance may well be declining.

Alongside the demonization of the male motorcycle club member, there has been a parallel historical development of women and their association with motorcycles. Owing to masculinist pressures on women, analogous to those exerted by social institutions on young men, women have found themselves in a peculiar relationship with their machines; the assumption that a woman riding a motorcycle exists in a 'deviant' category all her own, in which her sexual orientation – indeed, her general sexuality – is open to question and social comment. Responding to these pressures, women have either been (properly) oblivious, or insisted that in riding a bike a woman need not sacrifice her socially defined 'femininity'. The emergence of sportbike communities, and their gender-neutral (and gender-obscuring) protective clothing, seem to provide an opportunity for women motorcyclists, over time, to shed the social assumptions and personal anxieties about their identity as bike riders.

3 Images

From its inception, the motorcycle has been a distinctive element of popular culture: noisy, dangerous, exciting, eliciting the possibility of self display. Even *Tom Swift and his Motor Cycle* (1910) – a children's book and the first book on motorcycling ever published – depicts its hero deftly making adjustments to his motorcycle, enabling him to go faster, improve the engine sound or 'explosions', and enhance the menacing appearance of the bike (even though he's merely a boy!). Popular journalism of pre-war Britain portrayed motorcycles and their riders as menaces to polite society, noisy machines that frightened horses and disturbed the quiet British countryside. Photographs of Pancho Villa mounting his Indian or Che Guevara with La Poderosa only augmented the motorcycle's connection to rebellion and revolution, an image further cultivated in moving pictures as film offered more potent and enduring images of the biker as alienated, working-class 'tough guy'.

Scenes of Audrey Hepburn and Gregory Peck joyriding on a scooter in *Roman Holiday* (1953) may have conveyed the sense of liberation and escape commonly associated with two-wheeled travel – not to mention the stylishness of the Vespa – but neither its female princess nor the humble scooter became synonymous with motorcycling. Instead, a film appearing a year later introduced what was to become a recurring image of the motorcycle and its rider. *The Wild One* (1954) spawned dozens of American films – mostly from the American International Picture (AIP) movie factory – that exploited the menacing violence and sexual allure thought to be innate to motorcycle culture. British films from *The Leather Boys* (1964) to *Quadrophenia* (1979) pictured the conflicts between the Rockers and the Mods.

How are we to square such menacing, thuggish images of the motorcyclist with Robert Pirsig's inward, psychically conflicted journey in *Zen and the Art of Motorcycle Maintenance*? With Honda's 1963 ad campaign championing motorcycle riders as the 'nicest people'? Or Marianne Faithfull's portrayal of a sensuous female in 1968's *Girl on a Motorcycle*? Or the sexualized *She-Devils on Wheels* (1968) who ride their 'men as viciously as they ride their motorcycles'? Or the young urban, multi-ethnic sport-bike riders in *Biker Boyz?* Although the leather-clad prole may

Pancho Villa mounting his Indian.

have become an iconic image, a wide variety of other images exists of both the motorcycle and the motorcyclist, for both have protean significance in popular culture.

Motorcycles and motion pictures

Motorcycle and motion picture production emerged almost simultaneously. On 22 March 1895 Auguste and Louis Lumière screened *La Sortie des ouvriers de l'usine Lumière* (Workers leaving the

'The Flying Merkel': J. P. Schantin crossing the great American desert on his 'Flying Merkel' motorcycle, in 1913.

Lumière factory in Lyon), the world's first projected moving picture. At about the same time (1894) Comte Albert de Dion and Georges Bouton created the single-cylinder 125cc four-stroke engine that was to be the source of many of the world's first production motorcycles.

These two products of modern technology are linked more subtly owing to their relationship to motion and the perception of time. Film, quite simply, disassembles and reassembles time. The camera records a temporal sequence not by making a record of it, but by breaking time into a series of small, isolated and static moments, 24 times a second. Thus sundered, time is never really reassembled again, although most movies give the illusion of a forward temporal progression. By showing still photographs in rapid succession the movie projector fools our brain into thinking that we are witnessing a continuous temporal sequence.

Like the opening and closing of a film projector's shutter, which allows the film to advance through the projector (while keeping us in the dark for half the film's length), the opening and closing of a motorcycle's valves permit the introduction of fuel and evacuation of exhaust essential to the forward motion of the machine. Like the psychological illusion of motion caused by the rapid movement of still pictures through a projector, the rapid pace of the motorcycle through space not only thrills us but creates a psychological condition that is perhaps the one thing motorcyclists can agree on: riding a bike makes us feel free.

Early filmmakers sought to capture the heady experience of the new motorized vehicle. In screwball comedies the hero experimented with the chrome horse as a substitute for his trusty steed in chasing after his girl. Mack Sennett's *Love, Speed and Thrills* (1915) features a chase through the countryside on a motorcycle equipped with a sidecar, and in *Girl Shy* (1922) Harold Lloyd commandeers a motorcycle as well as many other vehicles en route to saving his girl. As a would-be detective, Buster Keaton makes a daring ride from a perch on the handlebars of a riderless motorcycle in *Sherlock Jr.* (1924). To rescue his love from kidnappers, he hops onto the bars of a bike ridden by his assistant, Gillette, who is almost immediately knocked off by a bump in the road. Keaton stays on, unaware there is no pilot, crossing busy intersections, riding along country roads, through construction, over a collapsing bridge, under a passing tractor and in front of an approaching train, stopping only when the bike collides with a pile of wood outside the kidnapper's lair. Obviously played for laughs, in these early comedies the motorcycle – like the girl – eludes the hapless romantic hero's control, its tantalizing wildness emblematic of his own unruly passion.[1]

From these beginnings, the motorcycle has become a staple of chase scenes in film, from romantic comedies to action dramas. While in the early screwball comedies the motorcycle took the hero toward his desired object, in later films the trajectory was reversed as the bike became a means of escape. In *Roman Holiday* Audrey Hepburn (as Princess Ann) flees the strictures of royalty and conventional femininity on a scooter. Like her screwball hero precursors, she too struggles to manage the novel device, uncertainly twisting the throttle as she careens through busy urban streets and up onto sidewalks. She is thrilled rather than alarmed as the vehicle transports her out of a confining traditional existence and into the arms of Gregory Peck. To much greater effect than *Roman Holiday*, however, Federico Fellini's *La Dolce Vita* (1960) made the humble Vespa not only stylishly modern but sexy. Hepburn's harmless ride with Gregory Peck takes place in broad daylight through populated Roman streets, while Anita Ekberg, blond hair tousled by the wind, clasps Marcello Mastroianni on a joyride under

the cover of darkness. Their ride carries the same sense of abandon and defiance of convention as Ekberg's midnight splash in the Trevi fountain.

It was not the sexy scooter but the more powerful motorcycle that made two wheels a staple of action films. Perhaps the most

Princess Ann (Audrey Hepburn) discovers the freedom of riding. Promotional still for William Tyler's *Roman Holiday* (1953).

famous motorcycle chase in film history remains Steve McQueen's ride on a Triumph twin in *The Great Escape* (1963). Playing American POW Captain Hilts, 'The Cooler King', he flees from his German captors by jumping his bike over a series of barbed-wire fences. Though based on a real incident that occurred on the night of 24 March 1944, the original escape did not involve motorcycles. They were added as a condition of McQueen's contract. He did the stunts himself, apart from the most daring 60-foot jump over the Austrian/Swiss border fence (which was performed by his friend Bud Ekins). Through the magic of editing, McQueen's chase is actually 'doubled', for, disguised, he also rides as one of his character's German pursuers. The spectacular sequence has inspired emulators in action films from *Mad Max II: The Road Warrior* (1981) to *Mission Impossible II* (2000) to *Matrix Reloaded* (2003). In *xXx* (2002), Xander Cage (Vin Diesel) reprises the famous *Great Escape* jump, succeeding where McQueen's character failed by successfully clearing the barbed wire.

Captain Hilts (Steve McQueen) on a Triumph twin near a border fence. Still from John Sturges's *The Great Escape* (1963).

The chase on a Ducati 996 in *Matrix Reloaded* may have eclipsed McQueen's ride in *The Great Escape* (although, given the excellence of the special effects in the *Matrix* film, it's difficult to compare the sequences head to head). Doubling for Carrie-Ann Moss as Trinity is Debbie Evans, the first female racer to compete at the AMA's 'Class A' level. A veteran of over 200 motorcycle stunt sequences, beginning with *Deathsport* (1978), she had already earned two Taurus World Stunt Awards for doubling as Michelle Rodriguez in *The Fast and the Furious* (2001). But her daring ride earned her another in 2004. Carefully choreographed, the sequence – part of an extended fourteen-minute freeway chase – first follows the bike as it plummets from the top of a tractor trailer, slips between two semis and cuts in and out of traffic across lanes and onto the shoulder, braking to a halt before almost colliding with a jack-knifing truck. The sequence then augments the sensation of the Ducati's speed by photographing the motorcycle racing not past, but *against* oncoming freeway traffic, showcasing its nimble handling (not to mention the stunt rider's skill) as it banks and turns abruptly to avoid collisions with other vehicles, finally exiting sharply down an entrance ramp. The

Trinity (Carrie-Ann Moss) on a Ducati 996. Still from Andy and Larry Wachowski's *Matrix Reloaded* (2003).

filmmakers took advantage of the fact that the chase occurs in the virtual world of the Matrix, employing a host of digital effects to heighten the experience. While Evans was filmed riding the Ducati against cars moving toward her, additional CGI vehicles were added in post-production to make the feat appear simultaneously more terrifying and exhilarating.

Synonymous with speed, the motorcycle has become ubiquitous in film, but only for limited sequences. Few films have focused entirely on the experience of racing. Notable are two British films: *No Limit* (1934) and *Once a Jolly Swagman* (1948). *No Limit* seeks to capture the excitement of the venerable Isle of Man TT races (and is still screened during race week). To convey authenticity, director Monty Banks used some of the first at-speed footage of bikes on the circuit and employed members of the Manx Motor Cycle Club in stunts. In *Once a Jolly Swagman*, Jack Lee used track-level camera angles to reproduce the spectators' view of seeing racers zip around a speedway. While both films featured the off-bike lives of racers, including their economic woes, the majority of the action takes place on the bike.[2]

Over half a century later, despite the growing preference for sportbikes among young riders, films still relegate racing to the margins (although documentaries such as *Faster* (2003) bring action movie techniques to a film about MotoGP during the 2001–02 seasons). *Biker Boyz* (2003) and *Torque* (2004) present scenes of amateurs racing against each other on sportbikes in the wee hours of the morning on near-deserted urban streets or groups halting daytime traffic to improvise circuits on highways. But this sort of competition is eclipsed by scenes of interpersonal antagonism and romantic rivalry. Even *Supercross: The Movie* (2005), directed by former Motocross racer and stuntman Steve Boyum, and featuring racers David Pingree and Tyler Evans, manages to reduce the

inherently visual appeal of the sport – the acrobatics and contact that make it a gripping spectacle – to a risible teen drama about mismatched brothers. Motocross, which subordinates speed to skill in negotiating terrain, lends itself not to long shots of speeding racers, but to slow-motion shots of bikes gone airborne or rear tires churning up dirt. The predominance of such images in televized sports coverage, however, has reduced them to cliché.

The reason for such failures may lie in the inherent difference between motorcycle and film. Motorcycling is essentially *embodied*, a physical activity felt in the body, through the smells, sounds and variations of temperature on the skin. Not only are the senses invoked, but keeping them sharp is one of the keys to survival on a bike. Movies, unlike motorcycles, do not invoke the sensorium. Movies are about sights and sounds, the eye and the ear, but there the sensory stimulation stops. The filmmaker can swoop the

Biker gone airborne.

camera along the sensuous lines of the machine, or pull back to capture it as it rockets past, but neither close-ups nor situating the bike on the road gives us any sense of being on the bike.

One solution, taken to thrilling lengths by some filmmakers, such as the *On Bike TT Experience* DVDs produced by Duke Video, is to mount the camera on the bike, sometimes one camera forward and one aft. At least then the sheer speed of the trees and rocks and walls as they rocket past us offers a degree of verisimilitude, as we can imagine leaning to the right and then the left along with the rider. But even this, despite its hypnotic attraction, fails to convey the totality of the experience of moving down the road, one with the machine. Film offers a mediated rather than an embodied experience. To be compelling, it needs to be psychologically convincing, immersing us vicariously in a simulation of the real thing. It appears, however, that film succeeds more often in involving viewers in narratives about people and their aspirations. As a result movies have tended to focus more on the biker than on the bike.

Bikers on the big screen

As we have seen, the now iconic image of the biker in *The Wild One* is founded on not one but two fictionalized portraits – one literary, the other photographic. Nonetheless, *The Wild One* and its spin-offs, such as *The Wild Angels* (1966), established riding as an act of rebellion against tradition and authority with obvious appeal to disaffected youths seeking thrills in the conservative 1950s. In *The Wild One*, the prim but attractive Kathie Bleeker (Mary Murphy) asks Johnny (Marlon Brando) in a moment of perplexity, 'What are you rebelling against, Johnny?' Brando, staring at his sternum in his best method acting mumble, answers, 'Whaddya got?' His words echo in Peter Fonda's speech in *The Wild Angels*:

We wanna be free! We wanna be free to do what we wanna do. We wanna be free to ride. We wanna be free to ride our machines without being hassled by The Man! . . . And we wanna get loaded. And we wanna have a good time. And that's what we are gonna do. We are gonna have a good time . . . We are gonna have a party.

As the film's title hints, the Wild Angels 'party' sensationally dramatizes the Sacramento funeral of infamous Hells Angel Jim 'Mother' Miles, killed after being hit by a truck in January 1966. Director Roger Corman sought to lend the film an air of authenticity by hiring Hells Angels from the Venice chapter as extras, but the film funeral presents luridly over-the-top images of bikers desecrating a church, engaging in sex behind the altar, toying with the body of their dead brother and then raping his girlfriend. The Hells Angels sued the film's production company, AIP, for defaming their image, even though it was unlikely that audiences – particularly drive-in crowds – saw it as anything other than a shocking spectacle.[3]

AIP and others were quick to exploit the bad-boy biker image, churning out a slew of films intended simply to titillate audiences with ever more salacious images. The titles alone give an adequate account of their formulaic content. Bikers are misfits and losers (*Born Losers*, 1967); lawless thugs (*Outlaw Motorcycles*, 1967; *Wild Riders*, 1971); inhuman 'savages' (*The Savage Seven*, 1968; *Savages from Hell*, 1968; *The Cycle Savages*, 1970) or, simply, evil (*Devil's Angels*, 1967; *Hell's Chosen Few*, 1968; *Satan's Sadists*, 1969; *Hell's Bloody Devils*, 1970). Predictably, many featured fictional Hells Angels (*Angels from Hell*, 1968; *Run, Angel, Run*, 1969; *Hell's Belles*, 1969) and, in a few, the real Angels were delighted to cash in on their own 'fame'. In *Hell's Angels '69* (1969), for instance, the 'gang' is played by the Hells Angels'

Oakland chapter, with Sonny Barger and Terry the Tramp playing themselves.[4]

Despite their claims to 'authenticity' the 1960s American 'chopper operas' or 'biker-sploitation' films bear little resemblance to the British biker films of the same era. The British Board of Censors banned *The Wild One* for fifteen years, thereby granting it the enhancing lure of the forbidden. Circulated through contraband prints, it influenced both motorcyclists and British filmmakers of the time, including Joseph Losey and Sidney Furie.[5] However, while films such as *The Damned* (1961) and *The Leather Boys* (1964) do similarly present bikers as anti-establishment rebels, they do so with a gritty realism that provides some insight into the origins, not simply the consequences, of youth rebellion.

Losey's *The Damned* features the 'Teddy Boys', children of servants who catered to the rich in seaside resorts such as Weymouth. Interestingly, while the other Teds wear the leather jackets popularized by Brando and his ilk, their leader, King (Oliver Reed), sports a mocking version of the upper-class uniform of tweed jacket and umbrella. The costume choice concisely conveys Losey's point: the young motorcyclists do not engage in violence simply for kicks or self-amusement but to assert power within a rigid class system that leaves them mired in poverty.[6] King concedes, 'I know it's kid stuff knocking about in a gang, but what else is there to do?'

Furie's film, another example of British realist or 'kitchen sink' films, features café racing not simply as a fad but as a means of self-definition and community-formation for impoverished youths lacking other means of social advancement. *The Leather Boys* offers realistic scenes of racing, using regulars from the Ace Café, including a 'burn' to Edinburgh through rain and fog. With equal fidelity it presents the hopelessness of a young couple who marry early, become disaffected with each other and seek comfort else-

where. Daringly for the time, the film briefly presents its protagonist Reggie (Colin Campbell) considering a homoerotic relationship with riding buddy Pete.

The Leather Boys focuses on the world of the Rockers on their café racers. Fifteen years later, *Quadrophenia* (1979) revived the supposed antagonism between the Rockers and the Mods. With its soundtrack taken from the Who album of the same name, the film reintroduced and reconfigured the scooter-motorcycle rivalry, through the character of Jimmy (Phil Daniels), who is slavishly devoted to his Mod buddies, preserving news clippings of their seaside brawls and seeking to emulate Ace Face (the musician Sting, in his movie debut), who rides

Ace Face (Sting) on his coveted Vespa. Still from *Quadrophenia* (1979).

the poshest Vespa. The film visually registers the differences in dress and even plays out the passionate divergence of musical preferences.

The Rockers earned their name from the Mods, who sought to disparage what they perceived as the bikers' hopelessly outmoded musical taste for rock'n'roll.[7] In fact, music was central to Rocker life, not simply as an aural sign of shared values, but as part of racing. A common feature of Rocker café society was making a 'record run': starting a record on the jukebox and heading out for a burn over a pre-arranged course, returning before the song ended.[8] The Rockers favoured musicians who sported their look and shared their interest in bikes: Elvis Presley (in the 1950s he owned a Harley-Davidson Model K Sport and he rode a Honda 350 Superhawk in *Roustabout* [1964]), and Gene Vincent, who had injured his left leg in a motorcycle accident at twenty. Their music captured the rebellious attitude of the young riders, even if it did not reflect motorcycle culture itself. Songs like the Crystals' 'He's a Rebel' and Shangri-Las' 'Leader of the Pack' (1964) now seem positively quaint, eclipsed by the 'wall of fuzz' guitar playing that became a staple of the biker-sploitation film soundtrack.

The nicest (or at least nicer) people

In the mid-1960s popular culture briefly gave the bad-boy biker of rock an image makeover. In 1964 the song 'Little Honda' by The Hondells hit number nine on the charts. Written by Brian Wilson, leader of the California group The Beach Boys, the song celebrated the small Japanese bikes beginning to enter the market. The chorus captures the fun of taking the bike up to speed:

First gear (Honda Honda) it's alright (faster faster)
Second gear (little Honda Honda) I lean right (faster faster)

Third gear (Honda Honda) hang on tight (faster faster)
Faster it's alright.

But the song's lyrics reassure listeners that the Honda's speed is
not menacing: 'It's not a big motorcycle / Just a groovy little motorbike / It's more fun than a barrel of monkeys'. Despite its small
size, however, it's (allegedly) better than a British bike:

It climbs the hills like a Matchless
Cause my Honda's built really light
When I go into the turns
Lean with me and hang on tight.

The song attests to the incredible marketing success of Honda
50s in America. In 1963 Grey Advertising created a campaign
designed to present riding a motorcycle as a benign and practical
activity. Ads with the slogan, 'You Meet the Nicest People on a
Honda', deliberately divorced the rider from the outlaw image pre-
valent in America. Featuring sunny photos of housewives riding on
errands, parents and children commuting to school, joyriding young
couples, grandmothers and even Santa Claus, the ads offered an
alternative image of motorcycling as safe, simple, fun and –
crucially for a Japanese company – all-American. In fact, the corporation became the first foreign company to sponsor the Academy
Awards and by the time The Hondells released their song a television commercial was airing across the country.[9] The campaign was
an astonishing success: in 1962 Honda sold 40,000 bikes a year;
by 1970 they were selling 500,000.

Other Japanese manufacturers were quick to emulate their rival,
enlisting fresh-faced celebrities to advertise their own models. A 1965
print ad for Yamaha's 'Riverside 60' features the stars of Disney's

That Darn Cat, Dean Jones and Dorothy Provine. Everyman Jones is pictured smiling broadly, sporting a turtleneck, red sweater and Hush Puppies, as golden girl Provine happily perches behind him in sunny yellow Capri pants and a matching sweater, fashions courtesy of the American department store Penney's. A basket mounted to the rear fender, containing 'that darn cat' and a box of Purina Cat Chow, further domesticates the motorcycle. The copy, though, reminds readers that 'beneath its rakish good looks beats a heart of pure *go* . . . sired by the World Grand Prix champion'. Although the engine is as 'quiet as a kitten's purr . . . it doesn't pussy

1963 advertisement, 'You Meet the Nicest People on a Honda'.

8:10 A.M. "Making a grand entrance is very important."

"Here I am arriving at the studio in style on Dean Jones' sleek new Yamaha "Riverside 60." The pretty girl is Dorothy Provine. Could you guess that beneath Yamaha's rakish good looks beats a heart of pure go...sired by the World Grand Prix champion? Anybody worth his catnip can tell you Yamaha's unique oil injection system and rotary valve engine give it an efficiency far superior to other sportcycles. You get maximum two-stroke economy (up to 200 mpg!) and don't have to bother with messy mixing of gas and oil. Of course, the engine's quiet as a kitten's purr. Yet it doesn't pussyfoot on power...whisks you along at 55 mph and never misses a lick. There's nothing common about a Yamaha. It's simply pure pleasure all the way!"

Get Going on the Greatest Going— **YAMAHA** INTERNATIONAL CORPORATION

© 1965 Walt Disney Productions

foot on power'. The ad promises performance and speed (55 mph) stripped of any association with danger or menace. It doesn't arouse disapproving glances or stares, but the reverse: a well-dressed black woman holding a soft drink in the background beams at a balding white man in white shirt and trousers passing by on the same model in blue.

Motorcycling appeared to have gone mainstream, recognized for what it was (and still is) in many parts of the world: a simple, fuel-efficient means of transportation. However, resting precariously on an image of American promise, this fresh-faced image of the bike

1965 advertisement for Yamaha's Riverside 60 featuring Dean Jones and Dorothy Provine.

and the biker was muddied at the end of the decade, as the emerging youth counterculture placed the motorcycle at the centre of both its definition and critique of freedom at home and abroad.

Transportation as transcendence

In films such as *Then Came Bronson* (1969) and *Easy Rider* (1969) riding the motorcycle is neither an ordinary, everyday experience nor an act of rebellion but a means of achieving freedom, of escaping from restrictions. In *Then Came Bronson* (which spawned an American spin-off television series in 1970) reporter Jim Bronson hits the road on his red Harley-Davidson Sportster after his best friend's suicide. Fed up with 'working for the man', he seeks peace and enlightenment in traversing America's open spaces. With no clock to punch, Bronson is free to roam, his trip leading to 'wherever I end up, I guess'. A peripatetic loner, he dispenses comfort and wisdom with the hippie catchphrase, 'hang in there'.

Released after *Then Came Bronson*, Dennis Hopper and Peter Fonda's classic road-trip film *Easy Rider* offers a more ambiguous take on the possibilities of transcendence through motorcycling. The film eschews racing through urban streets for long shots of riding on customized bikes through unpopulated fields and canyons of the American West. The individuation of the bikes, combined with iconic images of expansive landscapes under open skies, captures the optimistic desire for a new America, truly free and without prejudice. Riding chrome horses, Billy (Hopper) and Wyatt/Captain America (Fonda) are modern-day cowboys seeking less a physical than a mental or spiritual expansion through drugs. Their revision of Western myths is also figured spatially as they traverse the nation from West – California, where they seal a cocaine deal and secrete the cash in the stars-and-stripes gas tank

of Wyatt's chopper – to East, toward Florida and 'retirement' from the straightjacket of expectations and work.[10]

Steppenwolf's song from the film soundtrack, 'Born to Be Wild', captures the bike's centrality in fulfilling this heady promise:

Get your motor runnin'
Head out on the highway
Lookin' for adventure
And whatever comes our way
Yeah Darlin' go make it happen
Take the world in a love embrace
Fire all of your guns at once
And explode into space.

The trippy, psychedelic lyrics are fused to the 'heavy metal thunder' of the driving guitar and bass which replicate the rhythmic motion of the engine. The final verse transforms the machine into a vehicle for achieving a natural high and bodily transcendence:

Billy (Dennis Hopper) and Wyatt (Peter Fonda) traverse the American landscape on two wheels in a still from Hopper's *Easy Rider* (1969).

Like a true nature's child
We were born, born to be wild
We can climb so high
I never wanna die.

The song's hope for biker immortality makes it a nostalgic favourite at biker rallies to this day. In the context of the original film, however, the song's idealism is not sustained.

The film's original title – *The Loners* – underscores its emphasis on individual freedom and hints at the film's dark end. Before the two are shot by rednecks in a passing pickup, Wyatt had sensed the imminent demise not merely of their plans but of his generation's hopes for America: 'We blew it'. Their travelling companion, lawyer George Hanson (Jack Nicholson), had articulated the problem more concretely before his own fatal beating in an exchange with Billy:

George Hanson: You know, this used to be a helluva good country. I can't understand what's gone wrong with it.
Billy: Man, everybody got chicken, that's what happened. Hey, we can't even get into like, a second-rate hotel, I mean, a second-rate motel, you dig? They think we're gonna cut their throat or somethin'. They're scared, man.
George Hanson: They're not scared of you. They're scared of what you represent to 'em.
Billy: Hey, man. All we represent to them, man, is somebody who needs a haircut.
George Hanson: Oh, no. What you represent to them is freedom.
Billy: What the hell is wrong with freedom? That's what it's all about.
George Hanson: Oh, yeah, that's right. That's what's it's all about, all right. But talkin' about it and bein' it, that's two different things.

I mean, it's real hard to be free when you are bought and sold in the marketplace. Of course, don't ever tell anybody that they're not free, 'cause then they're gonna get real busy killin' and maimin' to prove to you that they are. Oh, yeah, they're gonna talk to you, and talk to you, and talk to you about individual freedom. But they see a free individual, it's gonna scare 'em.

Billy: Well, it don't make 'em runnin' scared.

George Hanson: No, it makes 'em dangerous.

The young men's senseless deaths invoke those of their real-life counterparts in the nation's internal struggle for civil rights and in the Vietnam War. The film's despairing ending suggests that complete transcendence through the motorcycle remains either a dream or a delusion.

Bruce Brown's documentary *On Any Sunday* (1971) mined the same naturalism to present motorcycling positively, as concrete physical transcendence and a wholesome activity for the entire family. The film featured dirt bike racing, which itself had been presented carefully and deliberately as a sport associated with health and athleticism. John Penton, one of the first importers of European dirt bikes to America, even avoided the word 'motorcycle', marketing his products as 'sport cycles' instead.[11] Edison Dye,

Family on a Sunday outing. Still from Bruce Brown's *On Any Sunday* (1971).

who imported Husqvarnas, circulated news releases claiming that Swedish researchers had determined that Motocross riders were some of the most physically fit athletes on earth.[12] Enlisting All-American actor Steve McQueen (who co-produced the film) to narrate, Brown offers motorcycle racing as an athletic challenge rather than simply dangerous, as good clean fun rather than menacing. *Dirt Bike* magazine, which premiered the same year, reinforced the message of the film: you could meet the nicest people not simply on a Honda but on any motorcycle.

The motorcycle's possibilities for human transformation were also explored offscreen, in literature. Robert Pirsig's memoir, *Zen and the Art of Motorcycle Maintenance: An Inquiry Into Values* (1974), made the bike central to a spiritual quest. Pirsig's book tells the story of a motorcycle journey from Minnesota to California with his son, Chris,

Actor/motorcyclist Steve McQueen on a dirt bike in Bruce Brown's *On Any Sunday* (1971).

but, as the subtitle announces, it is primarily an 'inquiry into values' and has little to do with bikes and even less to do with their maintenance. Instead, riding puts Pirsig into a meditative state that enables him to achieve insight. He notes that while riding in a car 'you're a passive observer and it is all moving by you boringly in a frame'. In contrast, 'on a cycle the frame is gone. You're completely in contact with it all. You're *in* the scene, not just watching it anymore, and the sense of presence is overwhelming . . . [T]he whole thing, the whole experience, is never removed from immediate consciousness.'[13] As a result, to Pirsig, the bike is a spiritual device: 'The Buddha, the Godhead, resides quite comfortably in . . . the gears of a cycle transmission as he does at the top of a mountain or in the petals of a flower. To think otherwise is to demean the Buddha – which is to demean oneself.'[14] Thus, in a brief span the author equates the bike with the self, and uses maintenance as a metaphor for self-reflection: 'The real cycle you're working on is a cycle called yourself.'[15] George Steiner's rapturous 1974 review in *The New Yorker* compared the book to another landmark in American literature:

> A detailed technical treatise on the tools, on the routines, on the metaphysics of a specialized skill; the legend of a great hunt after identity, after the salvation of mind and soul out of obsession, the hunter being hunted; a fiction repeatedly interrupted by, enmeshed with, a lengthy meditation on the ironic and tragic singularities of American man – the analogies with Moby Dick are patent.[16]

Even though the motorcycle is hardly the focus, the book remains one of the most popular books (allegedly) on motorcycling, having sold millions of copies in 23 languages.

The same might be said of Ernesto 'Che' Guevara's *Motorcycle Diaries* (made into a film *Diarios de motocicleta* in 2004 starring

Gael García Bernal). The book recounts the eight-month journey through South America undertaken in 1951–2 by Guevara, then a 23-year-old medical student, with his friend Alberto Granado on a 500cc Norton nicknamed 'La Poderosa II' (the Powerful One). As in Pirsig's book, the motorcycle journey is secondary to a spiritual awakening, not to Zen or the value of 'quality' but to the realities of poverty and illness in the developing world. Inevitably read retrospectively, with the knowledge that Guevara becomes 'El Che', the book is now mined for evidence of Che's nascent revolutionary politics. Contemporary journeys retracing Che's journey – from Patrick Symmes's *Chasing Che* to Barbara Brodman's *Looking for Mr Guevara*[17] – are motivated by the same desire: to find personal political inspiration.

Riders' and manufacturers' anxieties about distancing themselves from the 'biker' image attest to its remarkable power and persistence, not simply in America or Britain but in Slovenia or

'Che' Guevara (Gael García Bernal) and Alberto Granado (Rodrigo de la Serna) on 'La Poderosa II' (The Powerful One). Still from Walter Salles's *Diarios de motocicleta* (2004).

Latvia, where helmetless males in leather vests sporting their colours manoeuvre massive Harleys over cobblestone streets, tripping car alarms as they gun their engines and terrorizing pedestrians as they jump the curb to avoid parked cars. The distance the image has travelled comes not from the motorcycle but from the global spread of visual culture, particularly American popular film. Visual images do not require translation. The biker image – a fiction, not reality – nonetheless shapes perceptions of motorcyclists, affecting their self-presentation as well as the views of non-riders. From fictional boy hero Tom Swift to American late night talk show host Jay Leno, the 'biker' is leather-jacketed, male, white and, most often, heterosexual.

The other 'Angels'

By the late 1960s the hypermasculine image of the outlaw biker had become so ubiquitous that women's roles were reduced to two, defined solely in terms of their sexuality. They appeared either, like Nancy Sinatra in *The Wild Angels*, as the fawning and sexually available property of a male biker, simply another accessory to the motorcycle, or as sexually threatening and possibly emasculating or even castrating supervixens. The female riders in *She-Devils on Wheels* (1968) were advertised as 'Riding their men as viciously as they ride their motorcycles!' They have 'Guts as hard as the steel of their hogs!' The publicity for *Angels Hard as They Come* (1971) read, 'Big men with throbbing machines . . . And the girls who take them on'. *Angels' Wild Women* (1972) were equally 'hot, hard and mean . . . too tough for any man! They'll beat 'em, treat 'em, and eat 'em alive!' And in *The Mini-Skirt Mob* (1968), 'They play around with murder like they play around with men! They're hog strad-dling female animals on the prowl'. The tongue-in-cheek message here is that the films – like the very idea of women riders – should not be taken too seriously.

Even *Girl on a Motorcycle* (1968), directed by Jack Cardiff in the more realist style of British cinema, exploits the unbridled sexuality of its female star, Marianne Faithfull. The film takes its plot from a French novel (*La Motocyclette*, 1963) by André Pieyre de Mandiargues: the protagonist, Rebecca Nul, is a frustrated newly-wed, who takes flight on her Harley-Davidson, her 'black bull', to meet with her clandestine lover. Her motorcycle journey through Germany represents her quest for sexual freedom and personal fulfilment, underscored by the fact that she is naked under her leather suit. Visually titillating, the film lingers more on the protagonist's reveries en route to her lover than the activity of riding (which was done by male rider David Watson).

The army of gay/Nazi bikers in Kenneth Anger's cult classic film *Scorpio Rising* (1964) exploits the alternative sexuality of homosexual riders. While Furie's *The Leather Boys* had explored the very real homosocial possibilities inherent in male bonding through racing, Anger's film offered overtly sexual images of homo-eroticism largely divorced from the act of riding itself. Instead, the toughness and virility associated with the motorcycle was transferred onto hard-bodied, hypermasculine males posed in spiked leather and chains, iconography of the leatherman who became a staple of gay culture in the bars of New York and London and eventually a character in pop music's Village People.

The Village People's camp take on masculinity featured other iconic male heroes: a cowboy, an Indian and a cop. The cop might also have sported leathers for, historically, the military and the police have been quick to capitalize on the motorcycle's value as lightweight, manoeuvrable and fast. Filmmakers have recognized the narrative possibilities of presenting such service from the

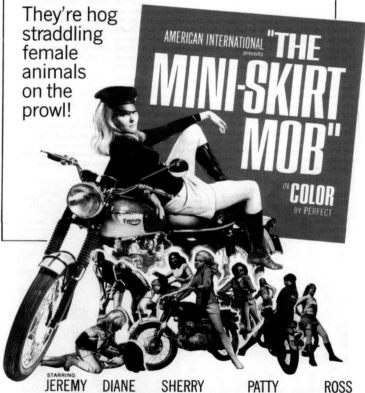

Poster for Maury Dexter's *The Mini-Skirt Mob* (1968).

rider's perspective. If the dominant film image associates motorcycling with delinquency and rebellion, a counter-image seeks to present the motorcycle and its rider as useful and disciplined, as an agent of the military or law enforcement.

Apparently inspired by Sonny Barger's bizarre offer to send the Hells Angels to serve in Vietnam, *Nam's Angels* (aka *The Losers*, 1970), draws on standard 'chopper opera' sensationalism, as Link (William 'Big Bill' Smith), a tough biker, is recruited by the US Army to rescue a CIA agent held in Cambodia. They trick out their Yamahas with guns and grenades to ride into the enemy camp, but are eventually killed, nobly sacrificing their lives for the 'man'.

With far more nuance, *Electra Glide in Blue* (1973) captures the life of Arizona highway patrolman John Wintergreen (Robert Blake). Rather than emphasizing the integrity and decency of the men in blue, the film conveys Wintergreen's discomfort in his role and on his mount, 'that elephant under my ass'. His partner Zipper embezzles money to buy his own bike. Unlike his colleagues, Wintergreen empathizes with the members of the counter-culture they revile. Filmed in Monument Valley (a visually evocative area in America's northern Arizona and southern Utah, made famous in the Westerns of director John Ford), it echoes not only the landscape of *Easy Rider* but its ending.[18]

Two-wheeled television

Translated to the small screen, the motorcycle has been tamed, its rebellious associations contained by television's need to appease advertisers by providing wholesome fare for the entire family. The dominant television genres – situation comedy and family drama – privilege interpersonal interaction, while the medium's limited use of action sequences reduces the opportunity to showcase the bike in motion. As a result, with few exceptions, the motorcycle is reduced to a prop and its rider co-opted for larger dramatic or comedic purposes in both fictional television series and their equally fictional counterparts, 'reality' television shows.

The long-running American television series *Happy Days* (ABC, 1974–84) is a case in point. Cashing in on the success of *American Graffiti* (1973), the show presented an unabashedly nostalgic portrait of the 1950s, stripped of any references to racism or bored, depressed housewives. Foil to all-American high-school student Richie Cunningham (Ron Howard) was Arthur 'The Fonz' Fonzarelli (Henry Winkler), a drop-out who rode Harleys and Triumphs, sporting the clichéd black leather jacket and motorcycle boots as visual evidence of his 'outlaw' leanings. While network suits were originally fearful of the jacket's 'delinquent overtones',[19] they need not have worried, for with his trademark thumbs-up 'aaayyh!' gesture The Fonz was no more a threat than Eric von Zipper, the hapless leader of the Rats in the Annette Funicello–Frankie Avalon beach movies.[20] Eventually, The Fonz became 'Fonzie', a big-brother figure offering advice about girls and even completing his high-school degree in night school.

Winkler's character may have been definitively reclaimed by suburbia in the animated series *The Simpsons*. In an episode aired on 28 November 1999, 'Take My Wife, Sleaze', dimwitted husband and father Homer wins a motorcycle and, after receiving a lesson in riding from son Bart, decides to form his own motorcycle club, Hell's Satans, oblivious to the fact that the name is already taken. The 'real' outlaws – Ramrod and Meathook (voiced by Winkler and John Goodman) – seek revenge by taking Homer's wife, Marge, hostage. Homer does eventually rescue her, but not before she has convinced Ramrod and Meathook to pursue 'a dream of a good job, a wonderful family, and a home in the suburbs'.[21]

In fact, animated productions in the UK, Europe and Asia have done more to deflate the iconic image of the bad-boy biker. Britain's lovable inventor Wallace and dog Gromit zip around on a motorcycle with sidecar in *A Close Shave* (1995) – just like the *Two Fat Ladies* did on their cookery programme. In Germany the loner outlaw of biker design, the chopper, has been reduced to a bumbling, unemployed, slang-wielding tinkerer who speaks in a near-incomprehensible North German dialect: Werner. Originally a comic-book hero, Werner has starred in four films: *Werner: Beinhart!* (*Bonehard!*,

Matakichi as a *bosozoku*.

1990), *Werner II: Das muß kesseln!!!* (*Eat My Dust!!!*, 1996), *Werner: Volles Rooäää!!!* (*Full Throttle!!!*, 1999) and Werner: *Gekotzt wird später!* (*We'll Puke Later!*, 2003). Part of his comic appeal lies in his persistent (and failed) attempts to manufacture two-wheeled creations out of ordinary household items and even vegetables, his rebelliousness reduced to stealing parts from other people's vehicles. The daring *bosozoku* have fared far worse. In the early 1980s, a photographer began photographing kittens standing upright in doll's clothing. One book featuring Matakichi (a female) traced her youthful experimentation with motorcycles and cars, parodying the *bosozoku* pilgrimage from adolescence to adulthood.[22]

Even the competing image of the motorcycle as an agent of the law received a sanitized treatment in America's *CHiPS* (NBC, 1977–83), following California Highway Patrol officers Frank Poncherello (Erik Estrada) and Jon Baker (Larry Wilcox) as they cruised the Los Angeles freeways on their Kawasaki KZ-900Ps and KZ-1000Ps. While the show did feature 'Ponch' and Jon at work chasing after speeding motorists or pulling over hijacked vehicles, much of the action focused on the contrast in personalities between the serious Jon and the fun-loving Ponch as they navigated the Southern California singles scene.

So-called 'reality' television has offered no less domesticated (or fictional) images. The genre's cinema vérité camera work has lured viewers with the promise of behind the scenes glimpses of custom fabrication in series such as *Monster Garage*, featuring Jesse James of West Coast Choppers, and *Biker Build Off*, pitting customizing icons such as Roger Bourget of Bourget Bike Works against young guns Eddie Trotta of Thunder Cycles and Billy Lane of Choppers, Inc. The most famous of all, *American Chopper*, offers voyeuristic pleasures of another sort. The show features Paul Teutul Jr, son of Paul Teutul Sr, who established Orange County Choppers in

1999 in Rock Tavern, New York, as an offshoot of Orange County Ironworks, his steel-fabrication business.[23] While Paul Sr does still create custom bikes himself, he serves largely as supervisor of the family business, with the work conducted by Paul Jr ('Paulie') assisted by his brother Mike ('Mikey'). While the sons are shown at work on bikes, their craftsmanship is not the focus. Instead, viewers tune in to see the family feud over their custom creations. Producer Craig Piligian, who also worked on *Survivor*, claims, 'This isn't a show about motorcycles. It's a family drama.'

Ewan McGregor and Charley Boorman's round-the-world ride in *Long Way Round* (2004) similarly focuses more on the friends' relationship, during their planning and on the road. If their intent had been to escape the press of stardom, as they recount in the book later published of their adventure, the presence of producers Russ Malkin and David Alexian, not to mention cameraman Claudio Von Planta, reminds us that we are watching a carefully orchestrated production rather than two blokes striking out on their own. There are sequences of the pair on two wheels, sinking into the mud on their heavy BMWs, slipping on stretches of sand, and other misadventures. But the series devoted more time to their off-bike adventures at border crossings, with shady Eastern European 'businessmen', and on the telephone with their distant family. Video-recorded 'diary entries' gave additional entrée to their thoughts about the trip and each other, once again making the human, and not his oneness with the machine, the dramatic interest. While ostensibly a documentary of their trip, the carefully edited narrative arc of the film follows the traditional fictional model of the quest tale.

The same occurs in the Canadian Broadcast Corporation (CBC) mini-series, *The Last Chapter/Le Dernier Chapitre* (2002–3), a thinly veiled portrait of the outlaw biker feud unfolding in Montreal from

1994 to 2001 as the Hells Angels and the Rock Machine battled for control of the illicit drug trade. In the series the Triple Sixers are seeking to extend their reach in Canada from their base in Quebec into the more prosperous neighbouring province of Ontario. Bob Durelle (Michael Ironside), boss of the Triple Sixers in Ontario, faces opposition from Montreal members, including Roots Racine (played by francophone rock singer Dan Bigras), as well as disgruntled members of his own organization, not to mention the Canadian authorities.

Obviously seeking to capitalize on the success of America's HBO Mafia-based series, *The Sopranos*, the series relegates motorcycling to the sidelines, focusing instead on organized crime. Like its American counterpart (and *American Chopper*), it devotes almost equal attention to the family drama unfolding within the Durelle household, as the wife objects to her husband's escalating involvement in drug dealing and murder. (In the opening scene Durelle excuses himself from a backyard barbecue with friends to assassinate a rival.) Tensions between the Montreal and Toronto leaders

Still from *Long Way Round* (2004).

also broadened the series' reach to Canadian politics, by invoking nascent and persistent divisions between French-speaking Quebec and the nation's predominantly English-speaking provinces.

Nonetheless, the series does provide insight into the hierarchical structure of post-war 'outlaw' motorcycle clubs, reinforcing their military origins by offering the police as a mirror image. Bob's nemesis is Bill Guénette (Michel Forget), the force's biker 'expert'. Not only, in classic detective-fiction fashion, is Guénette seen thinking like Durelle, he too faces opposition from within his own ranks. Both appear as veterans of a shared combat – against each other and against their young, more ambitious 'brothers'.

Changing images

Surprisingly, much mainstream television and film persists in showcasing the cruiser – either the Harley-Davidson marque or customized creations based on the same model – and sustaining the outlaw biker as the image of youthful rebellion, half a century after he first appeared in *The Wild One*. The 1980s film *Rumblefish* (1983), based on a young adult novel by S. E. Hinton and directed by Francis Ford Coppola, was among the first to challenge the legitimacy of the image. Rusty James (Matt Dillon) idolizes his older brother, known only as 'The Motorcycle Boy' (Mickey Rourke), and tries to inspire a revival of the 'rumbles' his brother led when he was younger. When his brother suddenly returns after a two-month absence, Rusty eventually recognizes that his idolized Motorcycle Boy is damaged – physically and perhaps mentally. If 'The Motorcycle Boy Reigns' (as graffiti on a wall proclaims) by the end of the film, it is only in Rusty's memory and imagination.

Over twenty years later, young rebellious riders now prefer sport bikes to cruisers. In fact, in *Biker Boyz* (2003) and *Torque* (2004), the once-iconic cruiser-riding outlaw biker is the stereotypical 'bad guy' rival to the sportbike riding hero. (The leader of the cruiser gang is musician Kid Rock, harkening back to the casting of Sting in *Quadrophenia*.) The menacing outlaw gang, older and white, resorts to violence, while the multi-ethnic sporty group demonstrates its power and superiority through racing. Bad-boy biker behaviour is no longer drinking, but popping wheelies in traffic or commandeering city streets for racing or making 'leaps of faith' from the pegs onto flattened gas tanks. Stunt riding or 'street bike extreme' is the new form of rebellion, inspiring a homespun guerrilla filmmaking movement that has found a home both in 'documentaries' and on numerous Internet sites featuring amateur stunt riding and the inevitable crashes.

Like skateboarders before them, young stunt riders film their exploits, using digital video broadcast instantly on the Internet.[24] Brit Gary Rothwell may have started the trend, having been 'discovered' by *Performance Bikes Magazine* performing stunts on his Kawasaki Z1300 at the 1992 TT. His skills were later showcased in two self-produced videos, *Showtime* (1995) and *Showtime II* (1998). In America, Ohio natives Scott Caraboolad, Kevin Marino and 'Big Dave' Sonsky styled themselves as the StarBoyz, compiling their own video titled *FTP 1*. (The group claims that the acronym stands for 'Full Throttle Performance', but, given the extreme nature of their stunts, many take it to mean 'Fuck the Police'.) No longer 'underground', if they ever were, the StarBoyz are now big business, selling T-shirts and other merchandise, promoting their 'Make Wheelies' school and advertising Suzuki as the 'StarBoyz bike of choice'.[25]

The most daring rider of recent film is not young, but old: 72-year-old eccentric and supremely gifted self-taught mechanical engineer Burt Munro, who set speed records in his native New

Zealand and in America, as well as being a competitive racer in Australia. Roger Donaldson, who had earlier produced a documentary *Offerings to the God of Speed* (1972), refashioned Munro's remarkable life for a full-length fictional film, the *World's Fastest Indian* (2005), starring Anthony Hopkins as a charming old codger who lives in a shack in Invercargill, the southernmost town on New Zealand's South Island, machines his own parts and won't give up on his dream to prove that his 1920 Indian Scout is the fastest bike on earth by testing it on the salt flats in Utah. The film collapses several trips Munro made to the Bonneville Salt Flats into one ride-of-his-life journey, encouraged by former racer Rollie Free, who had set his own record on the flats in 1948 on a Vincent HRD Black Lightning, wearing only a bathing suit. Emphasizing Munro's own unorthodox costume – battered helmet, wool sweater and rolled up trousers – and unorthodox bike, a decidedly quirky example of DIY ingenuity, the film presents both man and machine as endearing products of a simpler era and place, engendering the audience's support for his daring ride out of sympathy for the man rather than respect for his radical design or mechanical ingenuity.[26]

In recent fiction the rebellious biker is not a heterosexual male but a lesbian. Frankie J. Jones's *Midas Touch* (2002) revises the inward journey of the motorcyclist seen in Pirsig's book, *Easy Rider* and Che's diary, making the stakes not spiritual enlightenment or revolution but sexual identity.[27] Protagonist Sandra Tate embarks on her dream of 'buying a motorcycle and riding all over the country',[28] but only travels 275 miles, having discovered not only the lesbian mother she'd been separated from owing to her father's disapproval but a new lover. More famous are the illustrated novels forming the 'Mad Dog Rodriguez' trilogy – *Flaming Iguanas* (1997), *They Call Me Mad Dog* (2001) and *Hoochie Mama* (2001) – by author and cartoonist Erika Lopez, featuring Jolene Rodriguez, who

Two stills from *The World's Fastest Indian* (2005).

goes by her nickname 'Tomato'. Rather than simply offering an alternate biker culture run by women rather than men, the novels seek to revise motorcycle traditions themselves. The first book parodies outlaw mythology: Tomato and Magdalena form a gang called The Flaming Iguanas but, after an argument, each forms her own gang of one. A scene in the final instalment manages to poke fun simultaneously at Tomato, the myth of the consummately skilled rider, and bike manufacturers who cater to male bodies:

Cover of *Flaming Iguanas*, featuring 'Tomato' Rodriguez and her bike.

I flung my right leg over the seat, flicked up the kickstand, and well, there aren't too many bikes out there for shorter folks, and my yellowing bike is so big, I tiptoe when straddling it. What happened was I lost my footing on the cat litter on the sidewalk I had put down to soak up the oil from my last bike. My bike fell on my ankle before I could move it out of the way, and I was pinned to the ground.[29]

Billie Morgan, the title character of Jules Denby's 2004 novel, finds riding the key to escaping the confining grip of femininity imposed on her by her mother and sister, devotees of cosmetics and fashion. In the novel – presented as a memoir of her young adulthood in Britain's psychedelic 1970s – Billie recalls her first ride on the back of a friend's Bonneville:

Dusty assumed an expression of hard-nosed rebellion and gunned the engine in a fair imitation of Marlon Brando in the *Wild Ones* [sic] and I swung my leg over the seat and scootched in behind him, fumbling to hook my stack heels on the foot pegs he'd kicked down for me.

In that moment of seamless happiness, the smell of his sheepskin jacket mingling with engine oil and greasy denim, the liberating joy of being astride a machine that would carry you like Odin's eight-legged horse in a whirl of noise and disapproving stares from straight folk was beyond my wildest dream.[30]

Though she nearly falls off at first, she says, 'It was love at first ride, honest to God. I can still feel the sheer bliss of it. How brilliant it was, how *real* I felt as we chugged out of town towards home.'[31] Swooping around corners and past cars, receiving glares from startled drivers, she 'felt exhilarated' as if she'd 'been set free'.[32] Note that Denby's novel refashions elements of the male biker mythology – speed, rebellion, freedom – to describe one woman's coming of age.

A garage full of images

None of these contemporary images of the motorcycle and its rider dominates in popular culture, but together they offer an expanded, more diverse representation of motorcycle culture. They hold out promise for uncoupling the motorcycle from the dominant cultural images that have unfairly limited popular understanding of the bike and its riders, either demonizing or marginalizing them. In the past images oscillated between two extremes: the biker as mad, bad and dangerous to know, or the inverse, the motorcyclist was no different from your neighbour – far more likely to be the reality today.

Popular culture offers images of the motorcycle that are not simply mediated by the media of film, television, photography or music, but filtered through the lenses of public perception and their creators' imagination. It would be inappropriate, then, to identify the image as somehow accurately reflective of 'reality', since there isn't (and shouldn't be) any consensus on just what the 'reality' of motorcycling is, either among motorcyclists themselves (the ongoing and tedious discussions about what a 'real biker' is) or by the non-riding public (who are charmed by Johnny Strabler and the Fonz alike). Demographically, a 'real' biker in Europe or North America is probably a professional man in his mid-40s, but it would be a mistake to confuse a statistical majority with 'reality'. (Don't the majority of riders of two-wheelers live in the Third World, and ride bikes with 125ccs or fewer?) Instead, it's probably more useful to understand the image of the biker as a type of cultural currency, something that circulates among the media and citizens' imaginations, which has a reliably common value (the 'outlaw' biker is understood by everyone), but which functions not to identify members of a particular social group, but to embody a set of cultural values (rebelliousness, risk-taking, proletarian, etc.).

Attitudes of mistrust and fear in the 1950s and '60s gave rise to remarkably persistent images of the motorcycle as a menace and its rider as even more threatening, and the popular media either enhanced this image or sought to contain it.

These images can, however, collide with the real concerns of an individual, such as the female motorcyclist, causing her to fashion an image for herself (the 'lady biker') which is most appropriately contrasted not with other bikers, but with the image that the culture employs for the category 'biker'. The interesting thing here is not that the images are somehow 'not true' (they aren't) but that the images themselves have a real effect on people in the act of their self-fashioning. The Motor Maids spent real money on real clothing that identified them as 'ladies', based on opposition to an image of the biker outlaw that had no statistical reality in the culture, but was of immense value as cultural currency. So, the way to understand images is not to contrast them with 'the real', whatever that

Jimmy Murphy, winner of a 500-mile auto race at Indianapolis, Indiana, 30 May 1922, and Ernie Olson, mechanic, with the winning Harley-Davidson motorcycle.

is, but to seek to understand how images configure citizens' behaviour, and how in turn that behaviour alters the image or gives rise to a new image.

Perhaps the most popular contemporary image of the motorcyclist is the 'squid': the young, attractive but irresponsible sportbiker who is forever operating his machine just outside his skills. From California to Stockholm, everyone who rides knows at least one squid. Recent American films, with their worldwide cultural reach, have produced an image of this young man: attractive, skilled, tough, unafraid to use violence to defend himself, possessed of the talent to attract girlfriends who look suspiciously like runaway models. All over the world there are no doubt movie-going fourteen-year-olds who, in a few years, will sacrifice some of their limited capital to buy not a used Harley cruiser like Sonny Barger's but an aging R6 or a Ninja just like those cool dudes with the hot girlfriends in *Biker Boyz*. Sporting leathers and a helmet that matches

Representing demographic realities: professional men in their 40s. Still from Walt Becker's *Wild Hogs* (2007).

their bike, they can hit 80 in third, pop a wheelie, and say to themselves, 'Now I'm a *real* biker'.

Such contemporary images reflect changing attitudes accompanying the motorcycle's enhanced use and visibility as a mode of transportation. They focus less on the rider as a freakish outsider, offering instead insight into the range of motivations compelling them, from Burt Munro's passionate dedication to his old Indian to 'Tomato' Rodriguez's halting gestures at self-definition. Perhaps most significantly, such images recover the motorcycle, no longer relegating it to the background of the action or making it secondary to interpersonal drama but making it the heart of human endeavour.

The man-machine. Photograph by Gabrielle Keller.

4 Aesthetics

Beginning in June 1998, the Guggenheim Museum mounted a succession of motorcycle exhibitions in its museums in New York, Las Vegas and Bilbao, as well as the Field Museum in Chicago, the Wonders Museum in Memphis, Tennessee, and the Art Museum of Orlando, Florida.[1] This sequence of events produced a wide-ranging and fruitful discussion not only about whether motorcycles belong in a museum, but about the nature of art: art and non-art, high art and low art, art and craft, and so forth. One missing element in these discussions was the recognition that, within decades of their inception, motorcycles were not only already part of the artistic milieu, but considered to be on the vanguard of artistic expression: the Italian Futurists were in love with motorcycles.

Despite the historical significance of Italian futurism, it has received some deserved bad press. Its originator and principal spokesman, Italian Filippo Tommaso Marinetti (1876–1944), drove his artistic movement into a political corner with his bombastic and enthusiastic endorsement of Italy's nascent fascism. The Futurist Political Party, lasting from 1918 to 1920, was an incoherent mishmash of libertarian and authoritarian ideas. Despite its short lifespan and goofy ideology,

il Duce himself was prompted to exclaim, 'I formally declare that without Futurism there would never have been a fascist revolution.'[2] Before the decision to travel in this ignominious direction, however, Futurism did have something to say about the glory of an artistic movement founded on the wonder and excitement of speed.

Futurism has a pleasingly precise origin: the 'Manifesto of Futurism', authored by Marinetti and published in the Parisian newspaper *Le Figaro* on 20 February 1909. This artistic movement – primarily in fiction, poetry and painting – advocated speed, violence and warfare, new technology, the repudiation of history in general – and culture in particular – and the celebration of novelty for its own sake. However, this self-consciously 'modern' movement, originating in the mind of the wealthy, French-speaking, self-promoting Italian propagandist of Futurism, was not hermetically concerned with aesthetics. For central to Marinetti's vision was the marriage of the technological with the human, all for the glory of speed:

Motorcycle on display, *c.* 1914.

The world's magnificence has been enriched by a new beauty: the beauty of speed. A racing car whose hood is adorned with great pipes, like serpents of explosive breath – a roaring car that seems to ride on grapeshot is more beautiful than the Victory of Samothrace.[3]

Marinetti joyously encouraged his readers to turn their back on the past:

Set fire to the library shelves! Turn aside the canals to flood the museums! . . . Oh, the joy of seeing the glorious old canvases bobbing adrift on those waters, discolored and shredded! . . . Take up your pickaxes, your axes and hammers and wreck, wreck the venerable cities, pitilessly![4]

While there was some delight to be had in the negativity of destruction, for the Futurists genuine positive transcendence came from movement away from the past, a possibility physically incarnated in the new internal combustion machines – the airplane, the automobile and the motorcycle. These devices, which allow an individual to move faster than any personal conveyance since the chariot, can position us in another temporal category altogether: the future. This atomized individual man-machine, severed from the past and all its chains, as well as from contemporary society and all its entrapments, represents for Marinetti the birth of a new being, one who, in the starkness of his social and historical isolation, physically married to the machine, has at last become free.[5] For the motorcyclist, Futurism is historically significant in its recognition of how the bike's capacity to hurl us across the planet at great speeds results in a powerful, addictive side effect: the subjective sense of personal freedom.

Although violently rejecting romanticism (along with any other -ism that possessed any sense of an historical past), Marinetti's vision has clearly identifiable romantic properties, in particular the notion that 'freeing' one's imagination will in turn result in other types of freedom. Unlike the pastoral idyll of the romantics, however, Marinetti's freedom occurred not in a sun-dappled glen, but on a road, at the wheel of a powerful vehicle, hurtling through space at heretofore undreamt of speeds.[6]

Marinetti's creative impulses were largely manifested in prose.[7] However, the Futurist movement found expression in poetry, sculpture, architecture, the performing arts and elsewhere. While Marinetti glorified the motorcycle in his manifestos, the most striking display of Futurist ideas related to the motorcycle can be found in the work of visual artist Giacomo Balla (1871–1958).

Balla's early work was influenced by both Impressionism and Pointillism and was concerned with the effects of light in the intersection between perceiver and perceived. After sojourns in Rome and Paris in the 1890s Balla, born in Turin, returned to Italy and under Marinetti's influence signed 1910's 'Manifesto of the Futurist Painters' and 'Technical Manifesto of Futurist Painting'.[8] (It is worth noting that he named his two daughters Propeller and Light.) As a Futurist painter he continued his focus on the representation of perception, but concentrated on the visual analysis of motion. Probably his most renowned work is 1912's *Dynamism of a Dog on a Leash*. Like the other Futurists, his work celebrated the mechanical, in particular the motorcycle. His most striking image still clinging to representationalism is 1913's *Speed of a Motorcycle*. In the intersecting plane and semi-circles we can see what perhaps might be a motorcycle, but the viewer is left not with an image of the machine but the effects of the motorcycle's speed. Like the motion picture camera, this painting breaks a temporal sequence into discrete events. Unlike film, however, which fools the eye into the assumption of motion by showing a series of still photographs in quick succession, this dynamic image isolates, moment by moment, the viewer's apprehension of the motorcycle's motion, suggesting individual 'units' of perception by the eye and brain.

During the years 1913–14 Balla moved increasingly into complete abstraction, tracing an aesthetic shift analogous to that of his Impressionist colleagues. *Shape Noise Motorcyclist*, also from 1913, leaves the field of pictographic representation altogether, and instead offers the viewer a series of jagged polygons enclosed by a continuous, irregular spiralling line. The painting has lost some of the perceptual depth of *Speed of a Motorcycle*, but shares with it a set of flat, tempera colours: white, green, yellow-green and dark brown. The painting offers merely tenuous suggestions of

Giacomo Balla, *Speed of a Motorcycle*, 1913, oil on canvas.

the motorcycle's shape – the elements of the chain invoked by its cog-like arcs – and noise – the jagged edges of the white spikes evocative of the percussive sound of the engine. It is also possible that, like an Expressionist work, this painting evokes an inner state but, unlike the Expressionist who seeks to deploy emotion with paint in two dimensions, *Shape Noise Motorcyclist* suggests a pre-perceptual neurological event, prior not only to language but to perception itself. The legitimacy of such an interpretation depends on whether one assumes Balla is representing the experience of a spectator watching a motorcyclist, or the experience of the motorcyclist himself or herself. If the latter, Balla's Futurist vision could be said to anticipate the more modern psychological concept of 'flow' pioneered by psychologist Mihaly Csikszentmihalyi.[9]

As has been noted, motorcycling is a deeply embodied experience and its pleasures, like those of sex, are exceedingly difficult to communicate, whether through prose or visually. Part of the problem in communicating an experience on the motorcycle is that, owing to the need for total concentration and the necessity to draw on all one's driving skills to avoid danger, the reflective sense of 'me' as an individual disappears into the act of motorcycling. 'I' am no longer there when riding a bike; I have disappeared into the activity and become a man-machine. We call the basketball player who successfully shoots three-pointer after three-pointer 'unconscious' or 'in the zone' – he has lost all sense of self, and the ball just seems to leave his hands and go into the hoop. Correlatively, the motorcyclist, in giving over his or her total concentration to the act of riding, disappears into the ride. This experience is enormously exhilarating (motorcyclists call it 'freedom') but also incommunicable. This may well be the representational intention of Balla's painting and, as we shall see, it has implications for the question as to what extent the motorcycle is an aesthetic object.

One significant difference between the Futurists and motor-cyclists emerges in the Futurists' rhetorically violent rejection of the past in favour of the forward movement into the future (abetted by the novel internal combustion engine). By contrast, the male motorcyclist in particular, regardless of nationality, tends to draw on the American past as a model for identity. Through visual art and travel narratives, motorcyclists see themselves variously as medieval knights on a metal steed, cowboys on chrome horses, or riding with a tribe of brothers. The Futurists would, of course, forcefully reject linking their man-machine model with anything that was odiously historical and not 'modern'. For the Futurist, the man-machine unit defines us as a new kind of being, something transhuman in its unity between humanity and technology. Contemporary sportbike riders encourage this identification visually by wearing full leathers and a helmet that, to the spectator, visually meld them and the bike into a single unit. While this cyborgian understanding of the modern human lends itself more readily to science fiction than riding, there is unquestionably something to be said for the unitary experience of human-machine *flow* while riding a bike, a concept Marinetti would no doubt have endorsed.

However, the man who suggested we 'turn aside the canals to flood the museums' would be perplexed at the contemporary presence of motorcycles in museums worldwide. One of John Britten's motorcycles occupies pride of place in Te Papa Tongarewa, New Zealand's national museum in Wellington. It sits on a round metallic platform, lights glinting off its bright blue and 'Barbie' pink custom paint scheme. By accident, not design, it is only one of ten third-generation Brittens in existence, for its builder did not survive to see it enter into mass production, nor, it could be argued, did he ever intend his design to be replicated on a large scale. The bike, now a prized rarity, has acquired in New Zealand – and

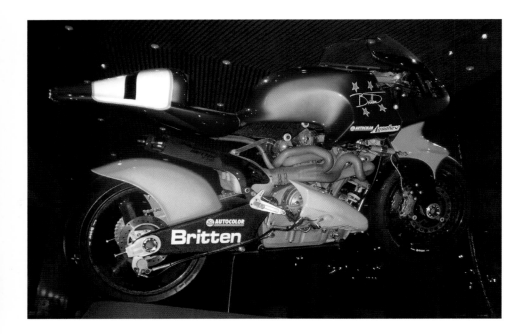

among motorcyclists – an iconic status as a cultural artefact of Kiwi engineering and motorcycle design, and as a beautiful object.

Even more surprising to members of the international art world was what occurred at the Solomon R. Guggenheim Museum in New York between 26 June and 20 September 1998. Spiralling up the ramp in the Frank Lloyd Wright-designed rotunda were 113 motorcycles – from an 1898 French steam-powered velocipede to a 1998 MV Agusta F4, with a gloriously varied array of other motorcycles in between. In place of the modernist works normally displayed in the museum were bikes spanning 130 years of technological development and design, neatly arranged on platforms against a curving metallic backdrop designed by Frank Gehry to convey their propulsive movement through space. Here was the motorcycle as art.

Motorcycle as art: a Britten V-1000 on display at New Zealand's national museum, Te Papa Tongarewa, Wellington.

The exhibition not only garnered a larger audience than any previous exhibition at the museum – over 300,000 visitors – but rivalled the yearly attendance figures for most museums world-wide. To date, not counting the Memphis and Orlando shows, over two million people have seen the exhibition. The catalogue for the show – not cheap in any currency – has sold over 250,000 copies.[10]

The show prompted discussion not only about motorcycles, but also about museums. What *was* a museum, after all, if it could exhibit motorcycles as art? Did a museum reflect culture or did it make culture? One possible rationale for the motorcycle's presence in the museum was to demonstrate various lessons about the larger culture, using the motorcycle as a stand-in for significant social events: the Vietnam War, the various revolts of the 1960s, etc. Or, one could claim (and this seemed to be closest to the Guggenheim exhibitors' intentions) that the motorcycle as an aesthetic object was a worthy object of visual contemplation in and of itself. Was the museum a place to display objects that reflected greater cultural concerns, or was it, to quote two museum critics, 'a place of struc-tured conduct in which behavior is targeted for ethical modi-fication', a place to regulate what counts as art and what does not?[11] If the latter, the Guggenheim was signalling to the rest of the world that it was reconsidering the question of what objects were appro-priate for an 'art' museum, that perhaps the distinction between art and design would have to be reassessed. This discussion tended to be centred not on what a museum is, but what art is (and, for that matter, what an 'art patron' is).

Critics' reactions served as a Rorschach test for what counts as art. Traditionalists sniffed at the burly, tattooed, jean-clad couples who patiently stood in lines that rounded the block. Others cele-brated opening the stodgy museum space to an entirely new demographic, patrons who might now be persuaded that museums weren't boring, dusty, airless rooms where paintings go to die. The mercantile observed that, like the exhibit or not, it pumped enormous sums of cash into museums, allowing the profits to perhaps be devoted to future showings of works unlikely to be seen otherwise.

Art theorists also got in on the act. Although theories of art are numerous and varied, tradition held with Kant's position that non-narrative art was art in its 'purposive non-purposiveness', i.e. something was art if it had no utility other than its sheer being. Clearly, motorcycles couldn't be art, and had no place in a museum, since they had an obvious purpose. Of course, from this point of view, architecture couldn't be art either.[12] Horace might come to the rescue here, with his understanding of art as *dulce et utile*, variously translated as sweet (or pleasurable) and useful. We could consider arts on a spectrum of sorts, those emphasizing pleasure and those emphasizing use. Kant's 'useless' arts would reside on the pleasurable end, while those that were undoubtedly pleasurable, but oriented toward use, such as architecture (and motorcycles) would find themselves on the other end of the spectrum.

However, we can (hopefully) cast these lengthy, theoretical and perhaps insoluble arguments behind with an observation from Chapter 1, that motorcycle design emerges historically with the transition to production vehicles. Even people who think that motorcycles are little more than devices created to promote organ donation agree that a motorcycle is a beautiful thing. And part of the bike's intrinsic beauty is that its utility, its purpose, is there for all to see: the most beautiful motorcycles are those from which everything has been removed except that which promotes and enhances the ride. If there are artists in the motorcycling world, they are the designers.

In general, design has to take into account a number of considerations, not least of which are the visual pleasures the object gives, and its use.[13] A harmonious design incorporates to the greatest extent all design considerations: for us a good design would be a beautiful bike that does what it's supposed to do, such as go fast or haul goods, bringing together the beautiful and the useful in one unit. Note, however, that in terms of comprehending what the motorcycle is a division emerges between the artist (designer) and the exhibitor. What the exhibitor has done is stripped the motorcycle of a crucial element, one which is forever atop both the bike and the mind of the designer: the rider.

The rider is, in the words of Bernt Spiegel, 'the upper half of the motorcycle'.[14] This is not only psychologically true, in riding as flow, but also valid from a design perspective. What the Guggenheim and other museums have done is portray the motorcycle as an art object independent of its purpose, modifying the viewer's orientation from utility (riding) to aesthetic contemplation. This is no small shift. The Guggenheim display, however successful, could only invoke or suggest the motorcycle's movement. In its transformation to a purely aesthetic object, the motorcycle was rendered static, immobile, deprived of the source of its motion: the rider. The motorcycle exists to move, to propel its rider down the road. And, while the visual design of a bike has an irrefutable allure, riding brings aesthetic pleasures appealing to all five senses. Each motorcycle comes to life with an affirming growl and opening the throttle releases distinctive aural signatures: the Harley V-twin's percussive 'potato, potato, potato', the quiet burr of a Japanese in-line four, the barely perceptible hum of a BMW. Riders feel the wind against their face and chest, the heady sensation of leaning while pressing their legs into the sides of the gas tank, the warmth of the engine rising up as speed increases. Smells of the road – hot asphalt, gasoline, brake fluid – mingle with fresher scents carried by country breezes of freshly mown hay and orange blossoms.

Capturing the aesthetic dimension of the motorcycle, then, means not considering its visual appeal alone, nor uncoupling it from its rider. Motorcycles, to be appreciated aesthetically, need to be ridden, when all our senses are engaged, not the least of which is the kinaesthetic. Severing the visual from the other senses is common enough in Western culture; 'aesthetic' derives from the Greek '*aisthesis*' (to perceive), but to understand motorcycle design in terms of its visual pleasure alone (while considerable) is to experience only part of the larger, holistic concerns involved, which include considerations of weight distribution, cornering ability, the ever-confusing rake and trail, sprung versus unsprung weight and so on. While such factors may seem to be more 'mechanical' or 'engineering' considerations, as part of industrial design, they ultimately serve not only the utilitarian aspects of the motorcycle, but its aesthetic dimensions as well, given that motorcycle aesthetics can only fully be appreciated while entering into a banked corner at speed.

Choppers

Ironically, motorcycle designs that sacrifice their utility in the name of beauty (and, from our perspective, fail to fulfil the minimal expectation of good motorcycle designs) have a disproportionately high visibility in contemporary culture. Choppers, unlike other motorcycles, are designed for pure display. Given the presence of choppers in contemporary popular culture, from Richard La Plante's narcissistic paean to the joys of paying someone to modify his motorcycle, in 1995's *Hog Fever*,[15] to the various televized chopper shows, the insect-thin, lavishly painted, jewellery-on-wheels moving spectacle, sporting a petrol tank that just might hold enough fuel to get you to the pub and back, the chopper represents a motorcycle to the general culture.

It wasn't always so.

Contrary to what the proliferation of reality television shows might suggest, this tendency toward customizing or 'chopping' is not a recent phenomenon but has been a practice as long as there have been motorcycles. The motorcycle itself was the serendipitous outcome, in a sense, of altering the bicycle by adding a motor. But such modifications were related to making a faster machine to propel humans along a road and can be distinguished from purely aesthetic changes. The lines have become a bit blurry, however. The rider who adds a Muzzy titanium exhaust to his Kawasaki Z1000, or a Yoshimura R22 Bling Stainless to her Hayabusa may not be primarily concerned with the fact that the exhaust pipe comes in carbon fibre or brushed steel, but you can bet he or she will take a moment to reflect on which matches his or her bike better. The Honda VTX rider, who already has 1800ccs of power and no real interest in pulling wheelies on a turnpike, chooses his Vance and Hines to fashion an aural image of himself as he cruises the streets.

Brian Klock, Klock Root Buell.

Some riders may argue 'loud pipes save lives', but the fact that they also grab attention and disturb the peace makes them more a reflection of the rider's favoured bad-boy biker image.

But 'chopping' first emerged among racers on dirt tracks. They cut or 'chopped' their rear fenders to prevent mud from building up under the wheel, which had an annoying tendency of stopping their forward motion. This was a practical solution to a utilitarian problem – getting the bike through the mud – but the practice has since evolved into one much more concerned with the 'look' of the bike, not so much as an object, but how the look reflects the personality and character of the owner. Chopped bikes are not objects of aesthetic contemplation, but stand-ins for their owners' self-image.

Another term for the utilitarian modification of a motorcycle was the 'bob-job'. So-called outlaws 'bobbed' their bikes – either shortened or removed the bike's fenders – and any other 'unnecessary trappings (saddlebags, windshields, chrome trim, big headlights) were chopped away'.[16] The original goal of bobbing was to improve performance by reducing weight and drag but 'a "bobbed" bike showed contempt for mainstream conventions and proclaimed the independence and individuality of its rider'.[17] Over time, the idea of modifying one's bike to reflect one's persona became de rigueur among members of motorcycle clubs. Bobbing one's bike not only reflected one's individuality; the various bobbing techniques testified to the owner's mechanical skill in welding, metalwork, mechanics and painting. A common term in motorcycle clubs for an unmodified motorcycle is 'garbage wagon'.

It has been argued that, like the original rationale for chopping – improving the bike's performance – modern chopping improves the bike's functioning. For example, lengthening the front forks adds stability on highways. However, the long front forks currently fashionable on custom bikes do not improve performance. In fact, the reverse happens. Their radical rake makes tight turns impractical, if not impossible. The lowered seat places the rider atop the engine's exhaust and, as customizer Billy Lane discovered firsthand, may make his seat (and pants) smoke in highway riding.[18] Extreme frame designs, pleasing to the eye, may require jettisoning shock absorption, submitting the rider to bone-rattling vibration. They may look stunning but are unlikely to outperform a 250cc scooter as dependable urban transport.

Instead, customizing can be seen, along with clothing and tattoos, as a form of self-expression. Creating a design from scratch or altering one's motorcycle to appear unlike others coming off the dealer's showroom sets it apart as a unique object reflective of the owner's identity and – in some cases – skill. It stresses the individuality of both bike and rider. As such, customizing is an extension of existing practices, in some senses nation- and/or class-identified. For instance, the Rockers who altered their café racers were, in part,

Making the bike your own.

expressing the British DIY ethos – 'Do It Yourself'. Those who make modifications themselves – rather than pay others to do it for them – demonstrate the ingenuity borne of having to make do, to fashion parts out of cast offs or rummage through junk yards for pieces to jerry-rig one-of-a-kind devices more out of necessity than design. This was the common practice of racing privateers who affixed aftermarket fairings and other parts to production vehicles.

In the American popular imagination, chopping reflects the ideal of independence. Captain America's bike in *Easy Rider*, for instance, with its extreme rake and miniscule, flag-draped gas tank, embodied the boldness and daring of a younger generation set on creating a nation free of prejudice and warfare. (Paradoxically, however, the film captures the contradictions of modern America.) The bike's radical styling turned the chopper into a symbol of both

Customizing sets you free. Still from *Easy Rider* (1971).

aesthetic and cultural rebellion, on the streets and especially in film, the ideal medium for making a dynamic visual statement. In *The Hard Ride* (1971), an otherwise forgettable 'bike-sploitation' film, the object of desire, Baby, is not a woman but an ostentatiously chromed chopper, coveted equally by biker outlaws, police officers and the priest who helped design her. The bike is – perhaps for the only time on film – the focus, in both narrative and visual terms. The camera pans up its radically raked forks (ornamented by three vertically stacked headlights), over its glittering pearlescent and gold gas tank, and lingers lovingly on its big shiny engine, before tracing the curves of its banana seat, supported by its preposterously elevated exhaust pipes. The film does remind viewers at various moments that Baby was the child of its owner, a black orphan raised in a white community, who created her with the help

Jerry Covington, Kids and Chrome Bike, 2006.

of a priest for whom customizing was a hobby and a humble, but talented, mechanic.

The current customizing craze, however, is no longer the bailiwick of average Joe tinkerers and hobbyist priests. It is the stage for a new breed of stars with celebrity clients from athletes Shaquille O'Neal and Lance Armstrong to less well-known but equally well-heeled private citizens. Customizers can now command well over $50,000 per bike and their products have been presented as artworks in a host of glossy coffee-table books, lit and posed like supermodels by a raft of professional photographers.[19] Featured in television series from *Monster Garage* to *Biker Build Off,* Jesse James of West Coast Choppers and the Teutul family of Orange County Choppers may sport the look and attitude of American labourers but they are, off screen, clearly millionaires, no different than the stars they design for (and, in the case of James, marry – he tied the knot in 2005 with Sandra Bullock). On the series themselves, their labour- and time-intensive craftsmanship is secondary to more viewer-friendly scenes of emotional display.

Another potential contradiction inherent in customizing is the predominance of the cruiser, particularly the Harley-Davidson brand, as the model of choice for chopping, invoking a certain regularity of design even among bikes designed to be individual. A glance down the line of competition-ready custom bikes at Daytona's Bike Week confirms the predominance of certain styles of customizing. Currently fashionable are long forks and fat rear tires, licence plate curved discreetly around the hub of the wheel.

Even custom scooters conform to some degree to this reigning motorcycle ideal. 'Chopper' scooters, fashioned primarily from Lambrettas, look like mini-Harley cruisers. Vespas with extra long forks can also become 'choppers', but their unibody design lends itself more to 'cut-downs', when the body panels are trimmed to make the scooter look slimmer. Even the Harley owners' predilection for chrome accessories has seeped into scooter culture. The contemporary 'Mod' scooters earn their name from their preference for 'modern' technological touches that reach back 30 years into the past: metal, mirrors and lights.[20]

In a culture prizing the visual appearance of bikes, scooter riders dismiss flawed examples as 'rats'. Still, with evident irony, some owners parade their dented, scratched and rusted vehicles at scooter rallies, like the 'rat bikes' exhibited at motorcycle gatherings, seeking attention and providing amusement. Whether lumbering Harley-Davidsons or wasp-like Vespas, motorcycles reflect the fashion sensibilities of their time.

Fashion

In the 1950s and '60s, artists, intellectuals and celebrities zipped from café to cinema on scooters, motorcycles that privilege aesthetics – not simply in the look of the vehicle but the sensibilities of its riders. A Moto-Scoot made the cover of *Cosmopolitan* magazine in 1937 and Salvador Dalí treated a sky-blue Vespa 150 as a canvas in 1962, painting his signature and the name of his muse, Gala, in gold on a side panel.[21] But scooters became a fashion accessory in the 1950s after Audrey Hepburn and Gregory Peck took a metallic-green Vespa 125 for a spin onscreen in *Roman Holiday*, with film stars Olivia de Havilland and Bing Crosby favouring the Salsbury Model 85 for its streamlined jet-age styling. With their step-through design and protective fairings, scooters allow riders to show off stylish suits, or dresses and heels, serving in effect as a moving fashion runway.

In fact, all motorcycles place not only their own design but their rider on display. If scooters can be said then to subordinate their own style to their riders, the reverse is often true for sportbikes.

Sportbike riders select full leathers and helmet in matching colours so that, in motion, they fuse with the bike in a blur of Yamaha blue, Kawasaki green or Honda red. While originally donned for protection against the elements and the track, the motorcyclist's leathers are now worn as much for display as for function.

This is most visibly evident in the iconic status of the black leather jacket – within motorcycle culture and, more significantly, outside it. The first motorcycle riders, cognizant that they, like the vehicle, were exposed to the elements, selected protective garb already in use for other outdoor activities. In the early twentieth century American riders on 'iron horses' borrowed duster-style jackets from their equestrian precursors, the cowboys, as defence against the wind and the dust kicked up by tyres on dirt roads. More intrepid adventurers dressed for combat. For her African crossing in the 1930s Theresa Wallach

Ray Weishaar, winner of the 100-mile race, Norton, Kansas, 22 October 1914.

donned desert fatigues and goggles. Later riders sought to emulate their kindred spirits in the pursuit of speed, aviators, sporting bomber jackets (which were derived from the uniform of cavalry officers).[22] British riders, for whom rain and mud were persistent nuisances, favoured foul weather gear such as Trailmaster and Barbour waxed-cotton jackets.

Such utilitarian concerns may have initially led riders to leather as the ideal fabric, as a durable and protective second skin. 'Why do motorcycle gangs wear leather?' an old joke begins. 'Because chiffon wrinkles so easily.' Leather is, in many ways, an ideal fabric for rider attire – it offers warmth, protection in the case of a slide on rough pavement, some defence against rain or debris – and, dyed black, disguises accumulated dirt. Racers still favour it, though their full suits are brightly coloured, not black.[23] Riders who do select gear for practical reasons are more likely, however, to order a Darien jacket made of 500 denier Cordura Gore Tex with a fleece liner and Scotchlite reflective tape in hi-viz lime yellow from the Aerostitch catalogue or a BMW Motorrad Club Jacket made of rugged polyamide impregnated for water resistance with removable safety armour in the elbows and shoulders. Modern fabrics – more lightweight, durable and waterproof – have supplanted leather for rider protection.

Instead, leather's popularity – for both riders and non-riders – stems from complex associations between the material, the machine and its riders. The black leather jacket became a talismanic token of toughness and masculinity through a combination of historical and popular associations. Recall that the Japanese *bosozoku* selected their colourful – and patently impractical – riding costumes to capture the boldness and brutality of samurai warriors and kamikaze pilots. The black leather motorcycle jacket also shares a military past, which explains in part why it is the choice of both outlaws and the police. It originated with German aviators of the First World War, such as Manfred von Richthofen, the famous Red Baron. Later associations with the Nazis further equated leather (and the colour black) with power and domination.[24] Some riders returning from military service after the Second World War did adapt their protective leather armour for the road. However, the connection is not through a direct association with war but rather mediated through fictionalized and sensationalized images of such ex-GIs in *The Wild One.*

The famous promotional still from the film displays Brando slouched confidently against his Triumph Thunderbird wearing a Perfecto 'One Star' jacket made by Schott. He wears leather gloves, jeans rolled up over boots and a military cap tilted at a rakish, devil-may-care angle. With his leather jacket zipped almost to the top, he exposes just a hint of neck. Ironically, just as the film did not reflect actual events in Hollister, California, Brando's uniform did not resemble actual biker wear. Many American riders considered his

WWII motorcycle jacket.

Leather-jacketed Johnny Strabler (Marlon Brando) in a still from *The Wild One* (1954).

pose effeminate and identified instead with the T-shirt-wearing Chino (Lee Marvin). Detached from actual riders or history, the jacket itself became an image resonant of rebellion, an attitude that could be purchased and worn – on or, more often, off the bike. The British manufacturer, Lewis Leathers, invoked unbridled power and speed in its model names: the Thunderbolt and the now iconic Lightning, 'magnificently made for the fast man', as one advertisement boasted.[25] The average male rider – no Boozefighter or Hells Angel (more likely a dentist or an accountant) – could feel masculine, sexually attractive and powerful simply by donning his jacket.

Commonly called a 'motorcycle' jacket, the garment retains vestiges of the machine's power and associations with masculinity derived from pre-existing equations of mechanics and speed with men. As an item of clothing, its intimate connection to the body further endows it with sexual significance. It represents virility – male potency and seductive strength. For this reason, both hetero-

Poster for Kenneth Anger's *Scorpio Rising* (1964).

sexuals and homosexuals have invested leather with a sexual appeal, an association that we've seen Kenneth Anger's cult classic film *Scorpio Rising* (1964) invoked and encouraged. The man featured in the film poster wearing a leather cap drawn down seductively over one eye bears more than a passing resemblance to Brando. In *The Leatherman's Handbook*, Larry Townsend explains, 'Intrinsic to the leather scene is the motorcycle and the guy who rides it. The clothing we all find so appealing is primarily designed for the cyclist's use.' He cites the 'sexual appeal of a leather-clad rider on his great rumbling machine. As a symbol of phallic might the motorcyclist is the epitome.' Note that Townsend does not say 'motorcycle' but 'motorcyclist', that the 'leather-clad' rider is the source of attraction, the leather jacket the real 'symbol of phallic might'.[26] For the same reason, leather is the fabric of choice for the whips, dog collars, belts and other props used to establish dominance in S&M rituals.

Women motorcyclists complicate this simple equation between leather and hard-edged masculinity. The Van Buren sisters were arrested several times during their cross-country ride in 1916 for wearing men's clothing. Other women who fear being considered mannish soften the dark ruggedness of the leather by selecting more 'feminine' colours, such as red or pink, or adding decorative touches such as rhinestones or fringe. The jacket then highlights the contrast between the masculine hardness of the leather fabric and their feminine softness.

Other women take advantage of this same contrast by wearing far less leather. Think Bike Week in Daytona Beach, Florida, with its parade of bikini-clad women wearing only leather chaps for coverage, or the ubiquitous 'booth babes' or 'umbrella girls' at MotoGP and Superbike events, sporting navel-bearing tops and tight leather shorts. They expose their sexuality not simply by

Woman in leathers, 1920s.

exposing flesh but by drawing attention to the contrast between the softness of their bare flesh and the toughness of the leather that partially conceals it. The interplay between leather and flesh adds to their allure.

This same contrast works when women wear full leather, especially if there is some suggestion of the flesh beneath. A tight leather suit, for instance, highlights the curves of the female body. A zipper open to reveal cleavage invites speculation about what else is hidden, an insight cannily exploited by the posters advertising the film *Girl on a Motorcycle* (1968), starring Marianne Faithfull. The X-rated version was called *Naked Under Leather* in America, Hollywood apparently quite willing to capitalize on the contrast. The poster recreates an early scene in the film that captures her pleasure in exploiting the contrast between the suit and her flesh: the camera focuses on Faithfull from above as she slips her naked body into the suit, then moves in from the front, lingering on her hand as she pulls the zipper up over her cleavage.

The fashion industry has also cashed in on motorcycle chic, transforming the material of masculinity into pricey items for feminine display. According to fashion historian Valerie Steele, couturier Yves St Laurent was the first designer to make leather stylish in the 1960s, but the 1990s may have marked the apex of the trend when *Vogue* magazine published a spread called 'Biker Chic' featuring a gaggle of supermodels wearing short skirts, clunky motorcycle boots, leather jackets and Brando-esque caps.[27] In the photo they stand closely together, blocking two motorcycles posed behind them, their wheels visible only at the edges of the frame. The motorcycles are completely beside the point, which is the sale of leather clothing designed by Claude Montana, Calvin Klein and others. No wonder that, in 1991, the Council of Fashion Designers of America credited Harley-Davidson for its influence on

Poster for Jack Cardiff's *Girl on a Motorcycle* (1968).
'Biker Chic', *Vogue*.

fashion. (Its highly successful MotorClothes division was launched in 1989.)

The motorcycle jacket has become so common in fashion design, in fact, that in 2004 it earned its own exhibit at the Phoenix Art Museum in Arizona. The exhibit surveyed how fashion designers such as Karl Lagerfeld, Roberto Cavalli, Moschino and Dolce & Gabbana have interpreted the 'look of the motorcycle jacket in their creations'. Note that while jackets themselves were on display – including one custom tailored for Elvis Presley – the focus was more on the 'look', on how the jacket has been reconfigured by designers. Another highlight of the exhibit was a Bob Mackie ensemble worn by Cher in Las Vegas in the 1980s, Swarovski crystals and all. In the words of the exhibit's promoters,

The October 2005 'Biketoberfest' motorcycle festival held in Daytona Beach, Florida.

'Here, biker style is off-road and center stage'.[28] Off-road indeed.

At this extreme, motorcycling is not merely influenced by but becomes style. The biker's leather jacket, uncoupled from the real risks of sliding on pavement, stands simply for toughness and 'cool'. Anyone with a credit card can walk into a local Harley-Davidson store, buy a branded jacket and acquire the cultural caché of riding. The motorcycle itself becomes a prop for advertisers of cameras or deodorant seeking to cash in on its edgy appeal – its associations with speed and modernity.

The bike featured now is not typically the cruiser associated with the dominant image of the leather-clad motorcyclist emerging in the 1950s. Instead, it is the sport bike, chosen for speed and associated with an altered image of the biker, the 'anti-chopper'. Uncoupled from its associations with a tough and rebellious male rider, the sportbike

The camera as motorcycle in an advertisement for Olympus cameras.

The motorcycle as accessory in an advertisement for Soft&Dri deodorant.

The anti-chopper.

evil. exquisite. exclusive. ECOSSE.

LUXURY AND PERFORMANCE UNITE in this surprisingly manageable street rod.
With no stretching, chopping or cutting allowed, The Heretic is a study in
refined aggression from years of precision engineering. Its meticulous
blend of exotic materials, unique styling and world-class, race-bred
components guarantee a riveting ride from stoplight to stoplight or through
the windiest canyons. Choose a riding style depending on your mood
with an ingenious **3 BIKES IN** 1 design. Simply adjust the suspension and
foot-control positions to move between hardcore road racer, plush cruiser
and wicked-low dragster modes. Any color. Any finish. Multiple options.
Limited to 100 custom, made-to-order machines.

ECOSSE
MOTO WORKS

exquisitely engineered for a fortunate few

TO ORDER
303.246.3080

VIEWS & PRICING
www.ecossemoto.com

'The anti-chopper'. Advertisement for Ecosse Moto Works, Inc. Cordero Studios.

appears to stand for speed and youth. It is the new fashion in motor-cycling. Advertisers are cashing in on its sexiness in a different sense – as new and popular, not necessarily erotic. (After all, deodorant is hardly sexy.) In fact, motorcycling itself has become fashionable.

Designers and design innovations

As commodities, motorcycles themselves are subject to changes in design determined at least in part by prevailing tastes and trends. Like their colleagues in the fashion industry, motorcycle designers become identified as particular individuals proffering a certain style. However, their skill involves more complicated considerations than draping the human body with cloth, combining complex issues of engineering and ergonomics with to-die-for visual style. Outside of fashion ads and museums, motorcycles are not static objects for visual contemplation. They move. The responsibility for creating a seamlessly attractive and useful machine rests in the hands of multi-talented artists: individual designers and design teams.

Indeed, the history of motorcycling can be written as a history of its myriad talented designers, from those who introduced a novel design element, such as Harley-Davidson's C. H. Lang, who in 1906 introduced the first clutch on an American motorcycle,[29] to New Zealand's John Britten, who designed every facet of his revolutionary 1980s racer. Certain motorcycles are associated with an individual designer, such as Max Fritz's R32 BMW Boxer, introduced in 1923 at Berlin's German Motor Show, or Charles Franklin's 1927 Indian Scout, or Edward Turner's Triumph Speed Twin, dating from the late 1930s. Other marques have enjoyed a string of successful designers, such as Royal Enfield, which employed such notables as Ted Pardoe, Tony Wilson Jones and Reg Thomas.

Some designs spring not from an identifiable personality, but from a design team. Yamaha, for example, has employed the GK Design Group. Originally a maker of organs and pianos, the Nippon Gakki Company was renamed the Yamaha Corporation in 1955. Responsibility for the design of its motorcycles fell on GK Dynamics, part of the corporate entity GK Design Group. Since that time, GK Dynamics has been responsible for scores of Yamaha products, from its original two-stroke 125cc YA1 to the 2006 1000cc in-line four Fazer.

Unquestionably, however, individual designers have left their mark on motorcycle design history.

Taglioni

One company well known for combining traffic-stopping beauty with track-dominating engineering is Ducati. Argentinean Miguel Galluzzi's design of the 1993 air-cooled, two-valve Ducati Monster has influenced the appearance of scores of subsequent naked bikes with its exterior tubular frame, the motorcycle equivalent of the Centre Pompidou. However, the company will forever be identified with a single designer, Fabio Taglioni (1920–2001), whose 35-year career with the company made his name synonymous with Ducati.[30]

Originally a producer of parts for radios, Ducati opened its first factory in 1935. The factory was destroyed during the war and Ducati looked for other products to produce. By 1946 the firm was marketing the Cucciolo, a kit to convert a bicycle to a moped and soon thereafter Ducati was producing the entire vehicle. A 175cc scooter was marketed in 1952, but Taglioni's arrival in 1954 dramatically changed the company's fortunes.

Having already designed bikes before arriving at Ducati, Taglioni came equipped with a vision of what a motorcycle could be. He is no doubt best known for his employment of the desmodromic valve. His

From imagining to fashioning. Photograph by Gabrielle Kelle.

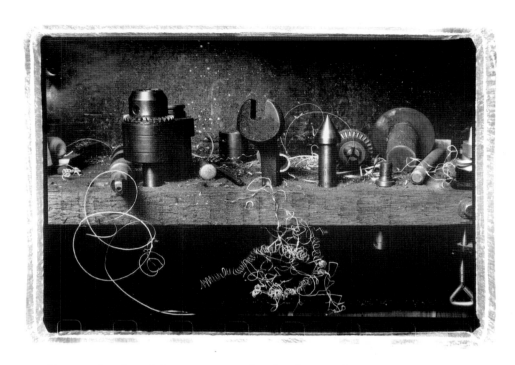

125 Desmo, developed in 1956–7, marks the first modern Ducati. Rather than use a spring to return the valve, the desmodromic system, originally using an additional camshaft, forces the valve back down, eliminating the spring and therefore problems such as valve float. Although not the first to use it, Taglioni proved that the desmodromic system could be employed in motorcycle engines that not only won races, but could, following adaptation, be sold to the public (in 1968, with the 450 Mark 3D).[31] Other models, with both twin and four cylinders, were to follow, resulting in Ducati race wins from Imola to the TT for Mike Hailwood, Paul Smart and Bruno Spaggiari. Ducatis acquired cachet equally on the basis of their racing pedigree and their distinctive sculptured 'jell-o-mold' gas tanks.

Tools of the trade. Photograph by Gabrielle Kelle.

Muth

The name of Hans Muth will forever be associated with the 1981 Suzuki Katana. However, Muth was by that time already well known as a vehicle designer. Along with co-founders Hans-Georg Kasten and Jan Fellstrom, Muth created products for Target Design, located in Seefeld, outside Munich, Germany. Having had experience designing automobiles, Muth was brought in by BMW to design a bike. The result was the 1973 BMW R90S, a 900cc Superbike, the first of BMW's line to break the 750cc barrier. The bike was introduced at the October 1973 Paris Show where, 50 years previously, BMW had introduced its first bike, the R32.

At 441 lb, with a top speed of 125 mph (sporting a five-speed gearbox) the R90S carried on the tradition of the venerable Boxer engine, created for long trips and a long life. Yet this was a seriously fast bike for its time and, in 1976, the third and final year of its production, Reg Pridmore won the first American Superbike Championship on a R90S, and the bike enjoyed additional victories at the Isle of Man TT and Daytona. What strikes the eye, however, is Muth's styling, most notably the 'bikini' faring housing the instruments and the two-seater 'ducktail' seat. The distinctive paint job, an airbrushed smoky silver and grey with pinstripes (in 1975 the base colour was orange), was executed individually; no two bikes left the factory looking the same. The R90S was followed by the equally popular Muth-designed R100S.[32]

Muth went on to design other bikes for BMW, including the R65LS. In addition, the Target Design studio continued to design motorcycles for various companies, among them Zündapp, Kreidler and, in one of their more striking designs, the Swiss motorcycle manufacturer Egli. However, there is little doubt that Muth and his Target Design team's most lasting contribution to motorcycle design was the Katana.

In 1976, feeling the heat from its fellow Japanese competitors, Suzuki introduced the GS-series of bikes, ranging in size from 400cc to 1000cc. A series of shaft-driven bikes followed. By the late 1970s, these 16-valve DOHC machines were extremely reliable, but too conventional looking. Two of Suzuki Germany's representatives, Otto de Crignis and Manfred Baecker, convinced management to contract the services of Target Design, using the GS1000E engine as a basis. Building on a design developed for MV Agusta, Muth and Fellstrom developed prototypes that went through two iterations: ED-1 (Euro Design) and ED-2. The latter grew into the GSX 1100S Katana, first shown at the IFMA Cologne in September 1980.

The most striking visual element of the bike is its wedge-shaped tank. Moreover, the tank itself forms part of a larger line commencing with the arresting fairing, moving along the gas tank, and

1973 BMW R90S, designed by Hans Muth.

flowing into the sculpted seat. However beautiful the lines, the Katana looks like many other contemporary bikes. But, of course, that's the point: the Katana's 'look', more than any other bike from that era, has influenced the design of many others, not just from Suzuki but from other manufacturers.[33] For its stylistic influence combined with its commercial success, the Katana has been called 'the most significant design of the last 50 years'.[34]

Britten

John Kenton Britten (1950–1995) and his design and fabrication team provided the world with one of the most exciting and beautiful race motorcycles ever seen, the Britten V-1000. Painted vivid metallic blue and bright pink, punctuated with swirling arterial Ming-blue exhaust pipes, the machine is gorgeous from any angle. More than a piece of sculpture, however, this mercurial machine was capable of crushing any bike in the world on the track, as it demonstrated on 7 March 1994, winning the Pro Twins race at Daytona, Florida, and other races from Pukekohe in New Zealand to Assen in the Netherlands.[35] The motorcycle press and Britten himself made it their business to portray the bike as originating from a DIY Kiwi puttering about behind the house and emerging with a powerful, distinctive vehicle. The truth was a bit different.

From the outset, John worked with other young men designing his bikes. The first important bike was the Aero One D, a 60-degree V-twin, using the engine as a structural member, designed with the help of friend John Brosnan (Broz) and modelled after a 1985 Grand Prix Yamaha.

Two things characterized the bikes Britten's team designed. In principle, they could crush anything that raced against them. In practice, the machines were bedevilled by mechanical problems

Britten, for speed. Putting function before art, the first prototype was tested on the Salt Flats in Bonneville, achieving a respectable 131 mph. But the bike was then bought by a Los Angeles car dealer who vowed never to start it again but just to look at it, privileging aesthetics once again. For Nesbitt and Confederate, however, the Wraith – as a kinetic sculpture – was meant to move, and production of a limited number began in New Orleans.

The company had planned to unveil its first ten production Wraiths on Halloween in 2005, but Hurricane Katrina decimated the Confederate factory. A belated celebration of sorts was held in January 2006 at the Ogden Museum of Southern Art at the University of New Orleans. At the exhibit, 'The Art of Rebellion: The Wraith', the motorcycle itself was not on display. Instead, Nesbitt's conceptual drawings and sketches filled the walls, in the absence of the tangible product they had created. The Confederate Motor Company has since moved to Birmingham, Alabama, and Nesbitt's designs still await realization.

Motion at rest: the Ecosse Heretic, Cordero Studios.

Poetry in motion

Shorn of its rider, the motorcycle can be contemplated as a thing of beauty. However, it challenges the traditional ideal of aesthetic contemplation, that of contemplative distantiation, for as an aesthetic object it is, as always, an element in a much greater nexus of cultural and social forces. As a museum artefact, it has undergone a contested redefinition (along with the concept of the museum's patrons). The artistry of chopping a bike has been transformed by the universe of television, which demands a melodramatic narrative alongside the exhibition of the mechanics' skills. The rider, donning protection against the dangers of the ride, finds himself or herself not only in the pragmatic world of self-protection, but in the world of seeing and being seen: fashion.

The motorcycle designer is in a position to acknowledge or ignore the larger world in his or her designs. Taglioni, with fashion in his blood, created fast bikes with an eye toward beauty that placed him firmly in the tradition of Italian industrial design. John Britten, schooled as an architect, produced a bike that polarized the biking community. With its pinks and blues and swirling pipes, the Britten showed the power of independence in approaching a design challenge. Hans Muth demonstrates how it's possible to toe the corporate line while creating an innovative bike whose influence has lasted for decades. JT Nesbitt shows how to be respectful of the traditions in motorcycle design while creating a bike that is totally of the moment. If the Guggenheim exhibitions introduced the concept of the motorcycle as an aesthetic object to the world at large, designers remind us that it has always been not only a vehicle for work and excitement, but an object of considerable and dynamic beauty.

Conclusion

The motorcycle has decidedly humble origins. The German Gottlieb Daimler simply wanted a means to test his engine. Carl Oscar Hendstrom, in America, created a pacer vehicle for his bicycle races. Decades later, Corradino D'Ascanio produced the Vespa owing to his dislike of the messy, noisy motorcycle. Yet, like the equally unpromising technology of cinema (Edison wanted a device to provide moving pictures to accompany his new and more exciting gramophone), the motorcycle eventually spread worldwide, becoming an integral part of the planet's economy.

While for a number of years the West dominated the production of motorcycles, exporting them to agricultural societies where they found their niche as work vehicles, those same developing societies found their way not only to be native producers of bikes, but also to continue proud marques, such as Royal Enfield. The populations of India, China and Japan displayed their ingenuity in not only adopting Western motorized technology but adapting it to their own needs and, as their economies grew, exporting motorcycles to the countries from which they originally acquired them. While those in Western countries most often see bikes through the lenses of popular culture, as masculinized symbols of rebellion, for most of the world a motorcycle is a practical, inexpensive means of transport. To understand the motorcycle as the consequence of purpose-driven design, we need to think globally, while riding locally.

Like other technologies, such as the computer, the motorcycle has spawned groups of like-minded people who, in gathering around their vehicles for exchange of information and amusement, engage in acts of self-definition and community formation. It seemed inevitable that whenever two motorcyclists found themselves together there was bound to be a race. These races now extend from the rural roads of the Isle of Man to the desert wastes surrounding Dakar. The proliferation of motorcycle racing and its effect on the development of motorcycle technology has been nothing short of remarkable. Racing around ovals or through village streets is understandable, but who could have imagined the existence, much less the phenomenal success, of sports such as Motocross and Supercross, where entire stadiums are filled with enthusiasts cheering on teenagers as they launch themselves from humps of dirt to fly through the air? Dog and horse breeders form associations around a specific breed, but consider projecting the development of clubs which have rigid rules of admission borrowed from the military, allow a member to ride only a certain marque (and not a particularly dependable one), deny females the right to participate, and dress in outlandish ways that strike fear in the hearts of others. There is no intrinsic connection between the 'outlaw' club and the motorcycle, yet not only did clubs thrive in America, but their popularity expanded worldwide, diffused, in part, owing to a technology that emerged alongside the motorcycle.

A low-budget film, spawned by a trivial incident in a sleepy California town in 1947, created the image of the motorcyclist that would endure for over 50 years, copied not only in film, song and story, but also by orthodontists on the weekend, as well as young

men everywhere, from Estonia to Vietnam. Women, largely unwillingly, were cast as minor characters in this masculinist drama, undoing decades of independence won by hopping on a motorcycle and leaving their parents, their husband, their town. With the rise of sportbiking, this image seems to be on the wane, but it also seems that as long as there are young men there will be umbrella girls whose sole function is to be part of the décor, or female passengers content merely to act as accessories to the bike.

The heart of the bike: the engine.

As riders and non-riders agree, the motorcycle, even shorn of its upper half, the rider, is a thing of beauty. While there are choppers built to look like rolling jewellery, motorcycle designers are well aware that the motorcycle, parked, resembles frozen speed. The bike's beauty can be fully grasped only when the rider is melded with it at 90 mph, tearing down a highway, but we are also asked to regard it in repose, from a distance, as an object of contemplation. Unlike the automobile, the motorcycle's beauty stems from its purity, from reducing the vehicle to its essential mechanical elements: an engine, two wheels, handlebars and a seat. Faced with the simplicity of such a transportation device, the design challenge is to preserve its naked functionality in a package that looks like it is already in dazzling motion.

Museums order not only the motorcycles into a comprehensive and comprehensible historical progression, but its visitors as well, directing and rationalizing their interactions with the bikes. Museum culture, turning its focus onto motorcycles, provides another way the machines can manifest themselves as cultural objects, subject to vicissitudes in taste and fashion. In turn, riders see themselves as an element of this aesthetic play, outfitting themselves to contrast with or merge with the machine.

Owing to their structure and the physics of motion, motorcycles, whether used for transportation or amusement, will always be seen as dangerous, especially in contrast to other modes of individual transportation such as the automobile. Yet, unlike other recreational activities that court danger, such as scuba diving or sky diving, riding a motorcycle can get you to work as well as give you a thrill. Socially, the question has always been who should best manage the risk associated with the motorcycle, a paternalistic government or the individual rider. As with most questions that centre on the tension between social costs and individual autonomy, the answer is a little bit of both. Requiring motorcycle education courses for new

riders, stiffening penalties for driving while intoxicated (hopefully for all types of vehicles), and perhaps a graduated licensing system for the young would preserve the motorcyclist's enjoyment of the freedom of the road while requiring that this beautiful machine be used responsibly. Given the physical danger motorcyclists face from automobiles, traffic-related injuries could be reduced further by educating automobile drivers that motorcycles are everywhere, and by disabusing the public that whenever a motorcycle is involved in an accident that the cyclist somehow has a greater responsibility for road safety than the automobile driver. The fear

Monument Valley, Utah.

Journey's end.

for motorcyclists' safety should inspire more education, not greater restrictions.

Ultimately, the designer is the core of the motorcycle. Design encompasses all the elements discovered later as the bike rolls off the showroom floor: performance, integration with the rider, dependability, susceptibility to modification, longevity and, of paramount importance, style. Increasingly sophisticated motorcycle design has make bikes more dependable, more efficient, and certainly faster, with some production bikes able to move down the road at 185 mph. Modern technology, from wind tunnels to dynamometers to computer-aided design, has enabled motorcycle designers to create virtual bikes in their studios, eliminating performance problems at the design stage and creating opportunities unavailable to mechanical tinkerers. Advances in materials technology promise to make bikes stronger, lighter and sexier.

Properly understood, the designer is the author of the motorcycle. Whether in a sophisticated corporate design studio or surrounded by like-minded amateurs in a shabby warehouse, the designer relies on a score of disciplines to breathe growling life and metallic beauty into what formerly existed only in his or her imagination. The result might be a unique, one-off bike or a consumer model that will be shipped around the world in the thousands. Designers began by bolting an engine onto a bicycle frame, and now they produce machines that, in addition to keeping the world of work in motion, find themselves in museums. Not for nothing has the motorcycle been called The Perfect Vehicle.

References

Introduction

1 James Boswell, *The Life of Samuel Johnson* (1791), Chapter 31.
2 Melissa Holbrook Pierson, *The Perfect Vehicle: What It Is About Motorcycles* (New York, 1997).
3 Thomas Haufe, *Design: A Concise History* (London, 1998), pp. 16–17.
4 Survey conducted in 2003 for the Motorcycle Industry Council by Irwin Bloch & Associates (of 2,000 households that own motorcycles/ATVs and 2,000 non-owning households).
5 Stephen L. Oesch, 'Statement Before the North Carolina House Select Committee: Motorcycle Helmet Laws', 4 March 2004, p. 3. http://www.iihs.org/laws/testimony/pdf/testimony_slo_030404.pdf#search=%22motorcycle%20demographic%22

1 Design

1 'MV Agusta F4 1000 Tamburini', MV Agusta, http://www.mvagustausa.com/web-mvagusta/F4-1000_Tamb.html
2 'Chinese Motorcycle Output, Sales Up', CRIEnglish, 9 February 2006, http://en.chinabroadcast.cn/855/2006/02/09/501@49016.htm
3 See 'Lifan', http://www.cartype.com/page.cfm?id=1424&alph=ALL&dec=ALL and Mohini Bhatnagar, 'Chinese bikemaker finalises entry plans', Domain-B: Indian Business, 22 January 2004, http://www.domain-b.com/companies/companies_l/lifan/20040122_entry.html. For the lf50qt-15, see American Lifan, http://www.americanlifan.com/lifan2/lf50qt-15.html
4 While some have speculated that the first bicycle-like device was sketched by either Michelangelo or Leonardo da Vinci in the fourteenth century, others have disputed the authenticity of the drawings offered as evidence. See Hans-Erhard Lessing, 'The Evidence Against "Leonardo Bicycle" Hoax', http://www.cyclepublishing.com/history/leonardo%20da%20vinci%20bicycle.html
5 The historical survey of bicycle development that follows is drawn from Fermo

Galbiati and Nino Ciravegna, *Das Fahrrad (Bicycle)* (Milano, 1989); Moritz Holfelder, *Das Buch vom Motorrad: Eine Kulturgeschichte auf zwei Rädern* (Husum, 1998); pp. 10–16; and the now definitive history by David V. Herlihy, *Bicycle: The History* (New Haven, CT, 2004).

6 Herlihy, *Bicycle*, p. 22.

7 Holfelder, *Motorrad*, p. 14.

8 Matthew Coombs, *Motorcycle Basics TechBook* (Newbury Park, CA, 2002), p. 37.

9 Bill Osgerby, *Biker—Truth and Myth: How the Original Cowboy of the Road Became the Easy Rider of the Silverscreen* (Guilford, CT, 2005), p. 14.

10 Herbert Wagner, *At the Creation: Myth, Reality, and the Origin of the Harley-Davidson Motorcycle, 1901–1909* (Madison, WI, 2003), p. 49.

11 Paul Heyd and Ernst Leverkus, *Motorräder: Geschichte & Geschichten* (Bietigheim-Bissingen, 1990), pp. 43–4. Kevin Cameron, 'FN Four', in *The Art of the Motorcycle*, ed. Thomas Krens and Matthew Drutt, p. 109.

12 Daniel K. Statnekov, 'Flying Merkel Model V', in *The Art of the Motorcycle*, ed. Thomas Krens and Matthew Drutt, p. 114.

13 National Highway Traffic Safety Administration (NHTSA), 'Motorcycle Safety', DOT HS 807 709, October 1999, http://www.nhtsa.dot.gov/people/injury/pedbimot/motorcycle/motosafety.html

14 NHTSA, 'Traffic Safety Facts: Motorcycles', DOT HS 809 908, 2004, http://www-nrd.nhtsa.dot.gov/pdf/nrd-30/NCSA/TSF2004/809908.pdf, p. 3.

15 Honda, 'Honda Develops World's First Production Motorcycle Airbag System', 8 September 2005, http://world.honda.com/news/2005/2050908.html

16 NHTSA, 'Traffic Safety Facts: Motorcycles', p. 3.

17 'The Airbag Jacket for Motorcycling, Horseriding and Power Sports', *Gizmag*, 17 March 2006, http://www.gizmag.com/go/4935/

18 Holfelder, *Motorrad*, p. 16.

19 Gary Stuart and John Carroll, *The Classic Indian Motorcycle: A History of the Marque, 1901 to 1953* (London, 1996), p. 30.

20 Didier Ganneau and François-Marie Dumas, *A Century of Japanese Motorcycles* (St Paul, MN, 2000), pp. 9–16.

21 For an engaging account of Yamaha's impact on Grand Prix racing, see Michelle Anne Duff, 'The End of Grand Prix Racing . . . Almost', *International Journal of Motorcycle Studies*, 1.1 (March 2005), http://ijms.nova.edu/March2005/IJMS_GstDuff0305.html

22 Heyd and Leverkus, *Motorräder*, pp. 35–6.

23 Ganneau and Dumas, *Japanese Motorcycles*, pp. 21–34.

24 Roland Brown and Mac McDiarmid, *The Ultimate Motorcycle Encyclopedia* (New York, 2000), p. 336.

25 '"Working Motorcycle Zone" Scores Big Hit at 38th Tokyo Motorcycle Show', http://www.jama-english.jp/motor/2004/200411.pdf

26 Colin Shattuck, *Scooters: Red Eyes, Whitewalls & Blue Smoke* (Denver, CO, 2005), p. 21; Peter Moore, *Vroom With a View* (London, 2003), pp. 160–61. The most

detailed history of the Vespa's development can be found in Davide Mazzanti, *Vespa: Style in Motion* (San Francisco, CA, 2004), pp. 28–40.

27 Mazzanti, *Vespa*, p. 17.
28 *Scooter! The Ultimate Guide,* Dir. Mark Cross (Duke Video, 2004).
29 Mazzanti, *Vespa*, pp. 100–105; Shattuck, *Scooters*, p. 25; Moore, *Vroom*, p. 72.
30 Mazzanti, *Vespa*, pp. 62–5.
31 Holfelder, *Motorrad*, p. 27.
32 Ibid., pp. 38–9.
33 We gratefully acknowledge Martin Rosenblum and the Harley-Davidson Corporation for this anecdote and the accompanying photograph.
34 Holfelder, *Motorrad*, pp. 64–68.
35 Janusz Piekalkiewicz, BMW *Motorcycles in World War II: R12/R75* (West Chester, PA, 1991), pp. 110, 180.
36 Ibid., p. 11. See also 'BMW History', Motorbike UK, http://www.motorbike-search-engine.co.uk/bmw_history.html
37 Mick Walker, *Royal Enfield: The Complete Story* (Wiltshire, 2003), pp. 24–6. Excelsior also had the Welbike, a 98-cc machine that could be dropped from the air. This bike, exported to the US following the war, and marketed in the UK as well, helped spawn the post-war interest in the scooter. See Peter Miller, *From Welbike to Corgi* (n.p., 1997).
38 Craig W. Floyd, 'A Record of Law Enforcement's Sacrifice during the Twentieth Century', http://www.nleomf.com/TheMemorial/Facts/CenturySacrifice.htm
39 T. E. Lawrence, *The Mint* (London, 1976), pp. 226–8.
40 Statnekov, 'Crocker', in *The Art of the Motorcycle*, ed. Thomas Krens and Matthew Drutt, p. 195.
41 'Osmos: La Roue Orbitale', http://www.osmoswheel.com/index.asp?lang=en
42 Phil Irving tells his story of the bike's development in 'The Black Shadow Story', originally published in *Two Wheels,* June/July 1973, reprinted at http://www.vincent-hrd.co.uk/story.html
43 Hunter S. Thompson, *Fear and Loathing in Las Vegas* (New York, 1971); *Fear and Loathing on the Campaign Trail* (New York, 1972); and 'Song of the Sausage Creature', *Cycle World* (March 1995).
44 Ted Bishop, *Riding with Rilke: Reflections on Motorcycles and Books* (Toronto, 2005), p. 15.
45 Melissa Holbrook Pierson, *The Perfect Vehicle: What It Is About Motorcycles* (New York and London, 1997), p. 21.
46 Roland Brown, *Superbikes of the Seventies* (Phoenix, AZ, 2002), p. 15.
47 Fermo Galbiati and Nino Ciravegna, *Das Fahrrad*, pp. 122–3.
48 For a popular exposition, see Jessica Marshall, 'Clean-burn Engine Dodges Ever Tighter Regulations', *New Scientist* (14 January 2006), pp. 26–7. The University of Cambridge Department of Chemical Engineering's 2006 paper is an example of current research: see Sebastian Mosbach *et al*, 'Simulating a Homogenous Charge Compression Ignition Engine Fuelled with a DEE/EtOH Blend', 2006, http://como.cheng.cam.ac.uk/index.php?Page=Publications&ID=SP-01-1362

For other sources, see the University of California, Berkeley, 'Homogenous Charge Compression Ignition (HCCI)', at http://www.me.berkeley.edu/cal/HCCI/, the US government's Sandia National Laboratory, 'Homogenous Charge Compression Ignition Fundamentals', at http://www.ca.sandia.gov/crf/research/combustionEngines/EGR.php and the US Department of Energy 2001 report to Congress, 'Homogenous Charge Compression Ignition (HCCI) Technology', April 2001 at http://www-erd.llnl.gov/FuelsoftheFuture/pdf_files/hccirtc.pdf. An interesting technical paper, Bengt Johansson, 'Homogenous Charge Compression Ignition: The Future of IC Engines?', sponsored by the Turkish Automotive Manufacturers Association, can be found at http://www.osd.org.tr/6.pdf

49 Bajaj, http://www.bajajauto.com/1024/index.asp

2 Identity

1 Ikuya Sato, *Kamikaze Biker: Parody and Anomy in Affluent Japan* (Chicago, 1991), pp. 146, 190; Karl Taro Greenfeld, *Speed Tribes: Days and Nights with Japan's Next Generation* (New York, 1994), p. 22.

2 Sato, *Kamikaze Biker*, p. 1.

3 Ibid., p. 41.

4 Ibid., p. 20.

5 Ibid., p. 43.

6 Ibid., p. 52.

7 Ibid., p. 24.

8 Johnny Stuart, *Rockers!* (London, 1987), p. 18; Bill Osgerby, *Biker—Truth and Myth: How the Original Cowboy of the Road Became the Easy Rider of the Silverscreen* (Guilford, CT, 2005), p. 116.

9 Stuart, *Rockers!*, p. 75.

10 Richard Barnes, *Mods!* (London, 1979), p. 8.

11 Dick Hebdige, *Subculture: The Meaning of Style* (London, 1979), p. 52.

12 Barnes, *Mods!*, p. 122. It is worth noting that the spotlight and mirror craze was just one of many scooter fashions. See Terry Rawlings, *Mod: A Very British Phenomenon* (London, 2000), pp. 145–7.

13 Zadie Smith, *White Teeth* (London, 2000), p. 23.

14 Ibid., p. 23.

15 Barnes, *Mods!*, pp. 11–15; Rawlings, *Mod*, pp. 11–41.

16 Stuart, *Rockers!*, p. 78.

17 *Sunday Mirror*, 2 August 1964, p. 13.

18 *Daily Mirror*, 3 August 1964, p. 11.

19 See Stuart, *Rockers!*, pp. 80–84; Barnes, *Mods!*, pp. 126–8; Rawlings, *Mod*, pp. 68–83.

20 Stuart, *Rockers!*, p. 83.

21 *Daily Mirror*, 3 August 1964, p. 3.

22 Chuck Zito with Joe Layden, *Street Justice* (New York, 2002), p. 51.

23 Accounts of the development of these clubs are numerous. Ralph 'Sonny' Barger, with Keith and Kent Zimmerman, *Hell's Angel: The Life and Times of Sonny Barger and the Hell's Angels Motorcycle Club* (New York, 2000); Yves Lavigne, *Hell's Angels: Three Can Keep a Secret if Two are Dead* (New York, 1987); Tom Reynolds, *Wild Ride: How Outlaw Motorcycle Myth Conquered America* (New York, 2001); Arthur Veno, *The Brotherhoods: Inside the Outlaw Motorcycle Clubs* (Crows Nest, NSW, Australia, 2002); Daniel Wolf, *The Rebels: A Brotherhood of Outlaw Bikers* (Toronto, 1991); Brock Yates, *Outlaw Machine: Harley Davidson and the Search for the American Soul* (New York, 1999); William L. Dulaney, 'A Brief History of "Outlaw" Motorcycle Clubs', *International Journal of Motorcycle Studies* 1.3 (November 2005): http://ijms.nova.edu/November2005/IJMS_Artcl.Dulaney.html.

24 Hunter S. Thompson, *Hell's Angels: The Strange and Terrible Saga of the Outlaw Motorcycle Gangs* (New York, 1966), p. 101.

25 Wolf, *Rebels*, p. 4.

26 Ralph 'Sonny' Barger with Keith and Kent Zimmerman, *Hell's Angel*, p. 254.

27 Osgerby, *Biker*, pp. 131–3.

28 The paper never actually ran the photo, suggesting 'the locals didn't consider Hollister a major story' (Osgerby, *Biker*, p. 31).

29 See Reynolds, *Wild Ride*, pp. 50–51.

30 Wolf, *Rebels*, p. 5; Lavigne, *Hell's Angels*, p. 29.

31 Dick Hebdige, *Hiding in the Light: On Images and Things* (London, 1988), p. 35.

32 Stanley Cohen, *Folk Devils and Moral Panics*, 1972 (New York, 2002), p. 6.

33 As one observer explains, 'if a robber has used a motorcycle to rob a bank, [the media] say, you know, "Motorcyclist Robbed a Bank" or whatever. They never say a motorist robbed a bank and, invariably most robbers are motorists'. See Suzanne McDonald-Walker, *Bikers: Culture, Politics and Power* (Oxford, 2000), p. 36.

34 Kate Flint, *The Woman Reader, 1837–1914* (London, 1995).

35 *The Motor Cycle*, 12 January 1904 (from the archive of Timothy Holmes and Rebekka Smith).

36 *The Motor Cycle*, 15 March 1904 (from the archive of Timothy Holmes and Rebekka Smith).

37 See Steve Koerner, 'Whatever Happened to the Girl on a Motorbike?: British Women and Motor Cycling between 1919–1939', *International Journal of Motorcycle Studies* 3.1 (March 2007), http://ijms.nova.edu/March2007

38 Marjorie Cottle, 'Motor Cycling for Beauty', *Evening Standard,* 25 September 1928.

39 Betty and Nancy Debenham, 'Motor Cycling for Health', *Daily News*, 16 March 1926.

40 Koerner, 'Girl on a Motorbike'.

41 Ann Ferrar, *Hear Me Roar: Women, Motorcycles and the Rapture of the Road* (North Conway, NH, 1996), pp. 22–3.

42 Wallach's journal accounts were finally published in 2001. See Theresa Wallach, *The Rugged Road* (Bucks, 2001).

43 Ferrar, *Hear Me Roar*, p. 35.

44 Brian Belton, *Fay Taylour: Queen of Speedway* (Lancaster, 2006).

45 In the 1930s, Stringfield mastered stunt riding at sixteen and then rode cross-country at eighteen. In honour of her efforts for both racial and gender equality, Stringfield was featured in the augural exhibit on Women in Motorcycle at the AMA Motorcycle Heritage Museum in 1990. In 2000, the AMA created the Bessie Stringfield Award to honour women leaders in motorcycling. In 2002, she was inducted into the Motorcycle Hall of Fame.

46 Linda Dugeau, *The Enthusiast*, April 1942, p. 17.

47 Ferrar, *Hear Me Roar*, p. 29.

48 'Motor Maids History', Motor Maids, Inc., http://www.motormaids.org/hist.html

49 Motor Maids, Inc., http://www.motormaids.org

50 Zito, *Street Justice*, p. 88.

51 Zito, *Street Justice*, p. 108.

52 'Dot Robinson,' Motor Maids, Inc., http://www.motormaids.org/dotlady.html. The title of Sasha Mullin's recent book, *Bikerlady* (New York, 2003), further suggests the persistence of this idea and anxieties about appearing inappropriately feminine.

53 Interestingly, like the Motor Maids, Dykes on Bikes has sought to trademark their name. Unlike the Motor Maids, however, they have met resistance, facing opposition based on their use of 'dyke'. See K. Alex Ilyasova, 'Dykes on Bikes and the Regulation of Vulgarity', *International Journal of Motorcycle Studies* 2.3 (November 2006), http://ijms.nova.edu/November2006/

54 Sirens Motorcycle Club, http://www.sirensnyc.com/

55 'Louise Sherbyn', WIMA Pioneers, http://www.wimaworld.com/

56 'About WIMA', WIMA GB, http://www.wimagb.co.uk/About%20wima.html

57 Kimberly Cosby, 'Challenging Stereotypes', *The Enthusiast* (Fall 2004), p. 30.

58 Christopher Thomas Potter, 'Motorcycle Clubs in Britain during the Interwar Period, 1919–1939: Their Social and Cultural Importance', *International Journal of Motorcycle Studies* 1.1 (March 2005): http://ijms.nova.edu/March2005/IJMS_ArtclPotter0305.html

59 McDonald-Walker, *Bikers*, p. 41.

3 Images

1 Art Simon, 'Freedom or Death: Notes on the Motorcycle in Film and Video' in *The Art of the Motorcycle*, ed. Thomas Krens and Matthew Drutt (New York, 1998), p. 69.

2 Mike Seate, *Two Wheels on Two Reels* (North Conway, NH, 2000), pp. 61–3.

3 The Hells Angels asked for $2 million; AIP settled for $200,000, and Sonny Barger subsequently worked on several other AIP films. The Oakland chapter play themselves in *Hell's Angels '69* (1969). The club also appeared in *Hell's Angels on Wheels* (1967), produced by a competing studio, US Films. Barger also served as 'technical advisor'. See Seate, *Two Wheels*, p. 24–6; Bill Osgerby, *Biker–Truth and Myth: How the Original Cowboy of the Road Became the Easy Rider of the*

Silverscreen (Guilford, CT, 2005), pp. 48–52.

4 In addition to Seate, *Two Wheels* and Osgerby, *Biker*, consult John Wooley and Michael H. Price, *The Big Book of Biker Flicks: 40 of the Best Motorcycle Movies of All Time* (Tulsa, OK, 2005). The book's subtitle is misleading for Wooley and Price focus almost exclusively on the 'biker-sploitation' films.

5 See Mike Clay, *Café Racers: Rockers, Rock 'n' Roll, and the Coffee Bar Cult* (London, 1988), pp. 29–30.

6 James J. Ward, 'A Contrarian Reading of Two Classic British Biker Films Joseph Losey's *These Are the Damned* (1961) and Sidney Furie's *The Leather Boys* (1964)', Popular Culture Association, San Diego, CA, March 23–6, 2005.

7 Johnny Stuart, *Rockers!* (London, 1987).

8 Stuart, *Rockers!*, p. 59; Osgerby, *Biker*, p. 118.

9 Honda Worldwide, 'History', http://world.honda.com/history/challenge/ 1959establishingamericanhonda/text08/index.html

10 On the motorcycle's significance in *Easy Rider*, see Michael J. Chappell, 'The Failure of the Flag in *Easy Rider*'; William Cummings, '*Easy Rider* and American Empire: A Postcolonial Interpretation'; and Greg Semack, 'What Happened to My Motorcycle Movie?', *International Journal of Motorcycle Studies*, 1.3 (November 2005): http://ijms.nova.edu/November2005/

11 By the 1960s, Europe excelled in producing dirt bikes, with major manufacturers in Spain (Montesa, Bultaco, Ossa), Sweden (Husqvarna), Germany (Maico), Austria (KTM, Puch), and Czechoslovakia (CZ, Jawa). See David W. Russell, 'The Dirt Bike and American Off-Road Motorcycle Culture in the 1970s', *International Journal of Motorcycle Studies* 1.1 (March 2005): http://ijms.nova.edu/March2005/ IJMS_ArtclRussell0305.html

12 Ed Youngblood, 'The Birth of the Dirt Bike: Technology and the Shift in Attitude toward American Motorcyclists in the 1970s', *International Journal of Motorcycle Studies*, 3.2 (July 2007), http://ijms.nova.edu/July2007/IJMS_Artcl.Youngblood.html

13 Robert Pirsig, *Zen and the Art of Motorcycle Maintenance: An Inquiry into Values* (New York, 1974, 1999), p. 12.

14 Ibid., p. 26.

15 Ibid., p. 325.

16 A copy of this review can be found at http://zamm.home.att.net/Reviews.htm. The website robertpirsig.org contains a wealth of information about the cultural and intellectual impact of Pirsig's notion of 'Quality'.

17 Patrick Symmes, *Chasing Che: A Motorcycle Journey in Search of the Guevara Legend* (New York, 2000); Barbara Brodman, *Looking for Mr Guevara: A Journey Through South America* (San Jose, CA, 2001).

18 Seate, *Two Wheels*, p. 74.

19 Mick Farren, *The Black Leather Jacket* (New York, 1985), p. 10.

20 As Lily Phillips notes, Eric von Zipper made the biker 'not only absurd, but what was worse, passé'. See 'Blue Jeans, Black Leather Jackets, and a Sneer: The Iconography of the 1950s Biker and its Translation Abroad', *International Journal of Motorcycle Studies*, 1.1 (March 2005). http://ijms.nova.edu/March2005/

IJMS_ArtclPhilips0305.html

21 'Take My Wife, Sleaze', *The Simpsons*, written by John Swartzwelder, directed by Neil Affleck, 28 November 1999.

22 Ikuya Sato, *Kamikaze Biker: Parody and Anomy in Affluent Japan* (Chicago, IL, 1991), p. 98. By contrast, journalist Karl Taro Greenfeld presents the *bosozoku* as not only still in action but firmly entrenched in the Yakuza world of drug dealing and theft in *Speed Tribes: Days and Nights with Japan's Next Generation* (New York, 1994). A documentary feature also called *Speed Tribes* was in production in 2003, and the director, Jamie Morris, collaborated with photographer Masayuki Yoshinaga whose book of photos appeared the same year: *Bosozoku* (London, 2002).

23 Osgerby, *Biker*, p. 160. See also Christian Pierce, 'Reality Bites Back: The State of Motorcycle Reality Programming in America', Popular Culture/American Culture Conference, San Antonio, TX, 2004 April 7–10.

24 See Michael Seate, *Street Bike Extreme* (St. Paul, MN, 2002), and Christian Pierce, 'Stupid Hurts: The Motorcycle Stunt Film Experience', Popular Culture/American Culture Conference, Atlanta, GA, 2006 April 12–16.

25 Starboys Productions, http://www.starboyz.com/

26 The film recalls the Irish film *Eat the Peach* (1986) also purportedly based on a true story. Two motorcycle enthusiasts – Arthur and Vinnie – lose their jobs when their Japanese employers decamp. After watching Elvis in *Roustabout* they are inspired to erect a Wall of Death thrill ride as a means of reviving their economic fortunes. As Seate notes, the film is 'more focused on teaching audiences about the importance of maintaining faith in one's dreams than any sort of statement of rebellion' (*Two Wheels*, p. 58).

27 See Sarah Boslaugh, 'Getting Past the Stereotypes: Women and Motorcycles in Recent Lesbian Novels', *International Journal of Motorcycle Studies*, 2.1 (March 2006), http://ijms.nova.edu/March2006/IJMS_Artcl.Boslaugh.html

28 Frankie J. Jones, *Midas Touch* (Ferndale, 2002), p. 88.

29 Erika Lopez, *Hoochie Mama* (New York, 2001), p. 117.

30 Joolz Denby, *Billie Morgan* (London, 2004), p. 58. The book was shortlisted for the 2005 Orange Prize for Fiction.

31 Ibid., p. 58.

32 Ibid., p. 59.

4 Aesthetics

1 The exhibits shared a core of motorcycles but were augmented by additional motorcycles and supplementary materials at each venue to reflect regional differences and the mission of each institution. On the significant differences between the displays at the Guggenheim museum in New York and the Field Museum in Chicago, see Mary K. Coffey and Jeremy S. Packer, 'The Art of Motorcycle (Image) Maintenance', *International Journal of Motorcycle Studies*, 3.2 (July 2007), http://ijms.nova.edu/July2007/IJMS_Artcl.Youngblood.html (forthcoming).

2 Emilio Gentile, *The Struggle for Modernity: Nationalism, Futurism, and Fascism* (Westport, CT, 2003), p. 41.

3 Filippo Tommaso Marinetti, 'The Founding and Manifesto of Futurism', http://www.futurism.org.uk/manifestos/manifesto01.htm

4 Filippo Tommaso Marinetti, 'The Founding and Manifesto of Futurism', http://www.futurism.org.uk/manifestos/manifesto01.htm

5 'Marinetti's emphasis on the "life" of matter was intended to obliterate traditional distinctions between the organic and the inorganic, between sentient beings and the physical and mechanical world. He sought, in poetry but also in art and in politics, to open a new field in which a chiasmic exchange of properties and attributes might occur. The Futurist male, "multiplied" by the machine, would exemplify a new superhuman hybrid adapted to the demands of speed and violence. Sportsman, aviator, or warrior, he would be capable of astounding feats of physical prowess. His inner consciousness, modeled on the running motor, would be emptied of all that was private, sentimental, and nostalgic – of all that in 1913 Marinetti called "psychology" – which he deemed a "dirty thing and a dirty word". Machines, in an inverse movement, would become the locus of all rejected human capabilities and drives, including libidinal desire and procreation' (Christine Poggi, 'Dreams of Metallized Flesh: Futurism and the Masculine Body,' *Modernism/Modernity* 4.3 [1997], p. 20).

6 Central to this idea is the 'pastlessness' of the experiencing subject: 'The triumph of the mechanical over the natural thus encapsulates the capacity of the modern subject to experience himself as pure origin, as uncontaminated by tradition' (Peter Nicholls, *Modernisms: A Literary Guide* [Berkeley, CA, 1995], p. 86).

7 Marinetti's ideas about prose can be found in two manifestoes, 'The Technical Manifesto of Futurist Literature' (1912), http://www.futurism.org.uk/manifestos/manifesto52.htm and, most important, 'Destruction of Syntax – Imagination without strings – Words-in-Freedom' (1913), http://www.futurism.org.uk/manifestos/manifesto08.htm

8 'Manifesto of the Futurist Painters', http://www.futurism.org.uk/manifestos/manifesto02.htm, and 'Technical Manifesto of Futurist Painting' http://www.futurism.org.uk/manifestos/manifesto03.htm

9 The principal discussion of flow can be found in Mihaly Csikszentmihalyi, *Flow: The Psychology of Optimal Experience* (New York, 1990).

10 Charles Falco, 'The Art and Science of the Motorcycle', http://www.optics.arizona.edu/SSD/aotm.html

11 Coffey and Packer, 'The Art of Motorcycle (Image) Maintenance' (forthcoming). Also see Steven L. Thompson, 'The Arts of the Motorcycle: Biology, Culture, and Aesthetics in Technological Choice', *Technology and Culture* 41.1 (January 2000), pp. 99–115; and Katherine Sutherland, 'Speed, Motorcycles, and the Archive' *English Studies in Canada* 30.1 (March 2004), pp. 73–85.

12 Craig Bourne, 'From Spare Part to High Art: The Aesthetics of Motorcycles', *Harley-Davidson and Philosophy: Full-Throttle Aristotle* (Chicago, IL, 2006), pp. 114–16.

13 Ashby and Johnson argue that there are six considerations in any design process:

market (needs/wants), investment climate (business strategy), aesthetics (industrial design), product use/disposal (specification), sustainability (environment), science (technology). See Mike Ashby and Kara Johnson, *Materials and Design: The Art and Science of Material Selection in Product Design* (New York, 2002), p. 8.

14 Bernt Spiegel, *Die Obere Hälfte Des Motorrads: Über Die Einheit Von Fahrer Und Maschine*, 4th edn (Stuttgart, 2003).

15 Richard LaPlante, *Hog Fever* (New York, 1995).

16 Bill Osgerby, *Biker—Truth and Myth: How the Original Cowboy of the Road Became the Easy Rider of the Silverscreen* (Guilford, CT, 2005), p. 26.

17 Osgerby, *Biker*, p. 26.

18 Episode 2 of the Great Biker Build Off series, pitting Billy Lane against Dave Perewitz, originally aired on American television on the Discovery Channel on September 1, 2003. Billy's radical decision to run the exhaust pipes underneath the seat and out through the fender resulted in his jeans catching on fire en route to the bike's unveiling in Texas.

19 Representative titles include *Choppers: Heavy Metal Art* (St Paul, MN, 2004) by Michael Lichter and *Extreme Motorcycle Art* (London, 2005) by Spencer Drate and Judith Salavetz.

20 Colin Shattuck with Eric Peterson, *Scooters: Red Eyes, Whitewalls, and Blue Smoke* (Denver, 2005), pp. 64–79.

21 His act inspired Art Vespa, an event sponsored by Vespa to raise money for Action on Addiction. In November 2004, contemporary British artists Gavin Turk, Gary Hume, Simon Peritone, Georgina Starr, and Harland Miller handpainted Vespa GTs for auction by Sotheby's. See http://www.britart.com/artvespa/

22 Rin Tanaka, *Motorcycle Jackets: A Century of Leather Design* (Atglen, PA, 2000). Tanaka traces the jacket's origins to around 1910, arguing that sports, not motorcycle, jackets were favoured until after WWII.

23 According to Tanaka, the change from black to bright can be traced to the 1960s, when Bates Mfg. Co. in Los Angeles introduced yellow and other colours. In the 1970s, the company led the way in producing high-performance racing suits.

24 Mick Farren, *The Black Leather Jacket* (New York, 1985), pp. 22–6. Farren also makes a more general connection between the cyclists' armour and that of the medieval knight (pp. 18–19).

25 Tanaka, *Motorcycle Jackets*, p. 203.

26 Larry Townsend, *The Leatherman's Handbook*, 1972 (New York, 2000).

27 Valerie Steele, *Fetish: Fashion, Sex and Power* (New York, 1996), p. 157.

28 Phoenix Art Museum, 'Motorcycle Jacket,' Fashion Design Gallery, 24 April–29 August 2004, http://www.phxart.org/pastexhibitions/motorcyclejacket.asp

29 Herbert Wagner, *At the Creation: Myth, Reality, and the Origin of the Harley-Davidson Motorcycle, 1901–1909* (Madison, WI, 2003), p. 90.

30 For the complete story, see Mick Walker, *Ducati: Taglione and His World-Beating Motorcycles* (Osceola, WI, 2001).

31 Ducati, '125 Triple Camshaft Desmo', http://www.ducati.com/heritage/anni50/125triple/125triple.jhtml

32 For information on the R90S, see Darwin Holmstrom and Brian J. Nelson, BMW *Motorcycles* (St Paul, MN, 2002) p. 92; Mick Walker, *History of Motorcycles* (London, 1997, 2000) p. 166; Roland Brown, *Superbikes of the Seventies* (Phoenix, AZ, 2002), pp. 76–81; and Mick Walker, 'BMW R90S', in *The Art of the Motorcycle*, ed. Thomas Krens and Matthew Drutt (New York, 1998) pp. 336–7.

33 For information on the Katana's development, see 'The Suzuki Katana', http://www.katanacentral.co.uk/; Peter Huppertz, 'GS: Evolution Perfected', http://www.thegsresources.com/gs_history.htm; and Clement Salvadori, 'Suzuki Katana', in *The Art of the Motorcycle*, pp. 348–9.

34 Glynn Kerr, 'Worth the Wait?' *Motorcycle Consumer News* February 2006, p. 38.

35 We are indebted to Tim Hanna's readable and exhaustive account, *John Britten* (Nelson, NZ, 2003).

36 Hanna, *John Britten*, p. 375.

37 Quoted in Larry Gould, 'Nowadays, behind even the most meticulously hand-crafted machine, is some high-tech design software', *Automotive Design and Production*, http://www.autofieldguide.com

38 Confederate Motor Company, 'The Art of Rebellion', http://www.confederate.com/home.html, August 2006. The site has since been revised to articulate the design philosophy of founder Matt Chambers, following its move to Birmingham, Alabama, after the company's factory was destroyed by Hurricane Katrina in August 2005. See 'The Post Katrina Team Confederate Design Manifesto', http://www.confederate.com/company.php

39 This account is drawn from Alan Cathcart, 'Wraith: The Art of Rebellion', *Motorcyclist*, April 2005, pp. 59–61; Mark Hoyer, 'Cutting Edge', *Cycle World*, April 2004, pp. 44–7; and personal communication with JT Nesbitt.

Select Bibliography

Appleton, Victor, *Tom Swift and His Motor-Cycle* (New York, 1910)

Ashby, Mike and Kara Johnson, *Materials and Design: The Art and Science of Material Selection in Product Design* (New York, 2002)

Baker, Christopher P., *Mi Moto Fidel* (Washington, DC, 2001)

Barger, Ralph 'Sonny' and Keith and Kent Zimmerman, *Hell's Angel: The Life and Times of Sonny Barger and the Hell's Angels Motorcycle Club* (New York, 2000)

Barnes, Richard, *Mods!* (London, 1979)

Belton, Brian, *Fay Taylour: Queen of the Speedway* (Lancaster, 2006)

Bishop, Ted, *Riding With Rilke: Reflections on Motorcycles and Books* (Toronto, 2005)

Bourne, Craig, 'From Spare Part to High Art: The Aesthetics of Motorcycles', in *Harley-Davidson and Philosophy: Full-Throttle Aristotle*, ed. Bernard E. Rollin, Carolyn M. Gray, Kerri Mommer and Cynthia Pineo (Chicago, 2006), pp. 101–16.

Brodman, Barbara, *Looking for Mr. Guevara: A Journey Through South America* (New York, 2001)

Brown, Roland, *Superbikes of the Seventies* (Phoenix, AZ, 2002)

Carroll, John, *The Motorcycle: A Definitive History* (New York, 1997)

Clay, Mike, *Cafe Racers: Rockers, Rock 'n' Roll, and the Coffee Bar Cult* (London, 1988)

Cohen, Stanley, *Folk Devils and Moral Panics* (London, 1972)

Coombs, Matthew, *Motorcycle Basics Techbook* (Newbury Park, CA, 2002)

Csikszentmihalyi, Mihaly, *Flow: The Psychology of Optimal Experience* (New York, 1990)

Denby, Joolz, *Billie Morgan* (London, 2005)

Drutt, Matthew and Thomas Krens, eds, *The Art of the Motorcycle* (New York, 1998)

Duff, Michelle Ann, *The Mike Duff Story: Make Haste, Slowly* (Ontario, 1999)

Farrar, Ann, *Hear Me Roar: Women, Motorcycles and the Rapture of the Road* (North Conway, NH, 1996)

Farren, Mick, *The Black Leather Jacket* (New York, 1985)

Fiell, Charlotte and Peter Fiell, *Industrial Design A–Z* (Cologne, 2000)

Frazier, Gregory, *Riding the World: The Biker's Road Map for a Seven-Continent Adventure* (Irvine, CA, 2005)

Fulton, Robert Edison, Jr., *One Man Caravan* (North Conway, NH, 1937)

Herlihy, David V., *Bicycle: The History* (New Haven, CT, 2004)

Galbiati, Fermo and Nino Ciravegna, *Das Fahrrad (Bicycle)* (Milan, 1989)

Ganneau, Didier and Francois-Marie Dumas, *A Century of Japanese Motorcycles* (St Paul, MN, 2000)

Gentile, Emilio, *The Struggle for Modernity: Nationalism, Futurism, and Fascism* (Westport, CT, 2003)

Greenfeld, Karl Taro, *Speed Tribes* (New York, 1994)

Guevara, Ernesto Che, *The Motorcycle Diaries: A Journey Around South America* (London, 1992)

Hanna, Tim, *John Britten* (Nelson, New Zealand, 2003)

Haufe, Thomas, *Design, A Concise History* (London, 1998)

Hebdige, Dick, *Subculture: The Meaning of Style* (London, 1979)

Heyd, Paul and Ernst Leverkus, *Motorräder: Geschichte & Geschichten* (Bietigheim-Bissingen, 1990)

Holfelder, Moritz, *Das Buch vom Motorrad: Ein Kulturgeschichte auf zwei Raedern* (Husum, 1998)

Holfelder, Moritz, *Motorradfahren* (Munich, 2000)

Hollern, Susie, *Women and Motorcycling* (New York, 1992)

Holmstrom, Darwin and Brian J. Nelson, *BMW Motorcycles* (St Paul, MN, 2002)

La Plante, Richard, *Hog Fever* (New York, 1995)

Lavigne, Yves, *Hell's Angels: Three Can Keep a Secret if Two are Dead* (New York, 1987)

Lawrence, T. E., *The Mint* (New York, 1936)

Lopez, Erika, *Flaming Iguanas* (New York, 1997)

—, *They Call Me Mad Dog: A Story for Bitter, Lonely People* (New York, 2001)

—, *Hoochie Mama* (New York, 2001)

Marriott, Paul and Yvonne Argent, *The Last Days of T. E. Lawrence: A Leaf in the Wind* (Portland, OR, 1996)

Mazzanti, Davide, *Vespa: Style in Motion* (San Francisco, CA, 2004)

McDonald-Walker, Suzanne, *Bikers: Culture, Politics, and Power* (New York, 2000)

McGregor, Ewan, Charley Boorman et al., *Long Way Round: Chasing Shadows Across the World* (London, 2004)

Moore, Peter, *Vroom With a View* (London, 2003)

Nicholls, Peter, *Modernisms: A Literary Guide* (Berkeley, CA, 1995)

Osgerby, Bill, *Biker—Truth and Myth: How the Original Cowboy of the Road Became the Easy Rider of the Silver Screen* (Guilford, CT, 2005)

Piekalkiewicz, Janusz, *BMW Motorcycles in World War II: R12/R75* (West Chester, PA, 1991)

Pierson, Melissa Holbrook, *The Perfect Vehicle: What It Is About Motorcycles* (New York, 1997)

Pirsig, Robert, *Zen and the Art of Motorcycle Maintenance: An Inquiry into Values* (New York, 1974)

Poggi, Christine, 'Dreams of Metallized Flesh: Futurism and the Masculine Body', *Modernism/Modernity*, 4.3 (1997), pp. 19–43.

Rogers, Jim, *Investment Biker: Around the World with Jim Rogers* (Holbrook, MA, 1994)

Sato, Ikuya, *Kamikaze Biker: Parody and Anomy in Affluent Japan* (Chicago, 1991)

Seate, Mike, *Two Wheels on Two Reels: A History of Biker Movies* (North Conway, NH, 2000)

—, *Street Bike Extreme* (St Paul, MN, 2002)

Shattuck, Colin and Eric Peterson, *Scooters: Red Eyes, Whitewalls, and Blue Smoke* (Denver, 2005)

Simon, Ted, *Jupiter's Travels* (Covelo, CA, 1979)

Spiegel, Bernt, *Die obere Hälfte des Motorrads: Über die Einheit von Fahrer und Maschine* (Stuttgart, 2003)

Steele, Valerie, *Fetish: Fashion, Sex and Power* (New York, 1996)

Steiner, Elfriede, *Ein Maedchen sieht Europa* (Vienna, 1956)

Stuart, Gary and John Carroll, *The Classic Indian Motorcycle: A History of the Marque 1901 to 1953* (London, 1996)

Stuart, Johnny, *Rockers!* (London, 1987)

Symmes, Patrick, *Chasing Che: A Motorcycle Journey in Search of the Guevara Legend* (New York, 2000)

Tanaka, Rin, *Motorcycle Jackets: A Century of Leather Design* (Atglen, PA, 2000)

Thompson, Hunter S., *Hell's Angels* (New York, 1967)

Thompson, Steven, 'The Arts of the Motorcycle: Biology, Culture, and Aesthetics in Technological Choice', *Technology and Culture*, 41.1 (January, 2000), pp. 99–115.

Townsend, Larry, *The Leatherman's Handbook* (New York, 1972)

Veno, Arthur, *The Brotherhoods: Inside the Outlaw Motorcycle Clubs* (Crows Nest, NSW, 2002)

Wagner, Herbert, *At the Creation: Myth, Reality, and the Origin of the Harley-Davidson Motorcycle, 1901–1909* (Madison, WI, 2003)

Walker, Mick, *Cafe Racers of the 1960s: Machines, Riders and Lifestyle. A Pictorial Review* (Trowbridge, 1994)

—, *History of Motorcycles* (London, 1997)

—, *Royal Enfield: The Complete Story* (Ramsbury, Marlborough, 2003)

—, *Motorcycle: Evolution, Design, Passion* (Baltimore, 2006)

Wallach, Theresa, *The Rugged Road* (London, 2001)

Warren, Lady, *Through Algeria and Tunisia* (n.p., 1922)

Wolf, Daniel, *The Rebels: A Brotherhood of Outlaw Bikers* (Toronto, 1991)

Wood, John, 'Hell's Angels and the Illusion of the Counterculture', *The Journal of Popular Culture*, 37.2 (2003), pp. 336–51.

Wooley, John and Michael H. Price, *The Big Book of Biker Flicks: 40 of the Best Motorcycle Movies of All Time* (Tulsa, OK, 2005)

Zito, Chuck and Joe Layden, *Street Justice* (New York, 2002)

Acknowledgements

Books are made not only by authors but with the indispensable help of friends, relatives, experts, editors and the odd person you meet while on the road. Our book would not have been possible without our best riding buddies, Barbara Brodman and Chachi Pacheco in the US and Geoff and Cynthia Crowther in the UK, and our own ever-expanding international community of biker intellectuals and intellectual bikers, including Greg Horne, Alice Sexton, Wendy Moon, Gary Kieffner, Tim Holmes, Katherine Sutherland, Randy McBee, Michael Chappell, Christian Pierce, Jessica Keesee, Rich Remsberg, Matthew Linton, Jim Ward, Kris Slawinski and, especially, Ted Bishop, who recommended this project to us. Mallory Young, Tim Holmes and Katherine Sutherland kindly read drafts of portions of this work and offered sage advice and gentle correction. We would also like to recognize Don Rosenblum, Dean of the Farquhar College of Arts and Sciences at Nova Southeastern University, for his timely and enthusiastic support. For considering motorcycle culture an integral part of popular culture, we are grateful to Leslie Fife, Program Coordinator of the Popular Culture/American Culture conference, and Professor Gerd Hurm, founder and director of the Trier Center for American Studies in Germany. We would also like to thank our non-riding friends and family, who have supported and encouraged us, even pretending enthusiasm while viewing hundreds of photographs of shiny motorcycles.

Photographic Acknowledgements

The author and publishers wish to express their thanks to the below sources of illustrative material and/or permission to reproduce it:

photos Alexander Turnbull Library, Wellington, New Zealand: pp. 22 (Steffano Webb Collection), 35 (B. Davis Collection), 58, 68 (top), 162 (F. N. Jones Collection), 186 (*Evening Post* Collection); photos courtesy of American Honda Motor Co., Inc.: pp. 40, 52 (foot), 56, 133; used by kind permission of American Lifan Industry, Inc. (Dallas, Texas): p. 14 (foot); photo courtesy of BMW of North America: p. 197; photos Columbia Pictures/Photofest: pp. 136, 176; photo Courtesy of Confederate Motor Company: p. 202; photos Cordero Studios, courtesy of Ecosse Moto Works, Inc.: pp. 191, 203; photo Focus Features/Photofest: 141; Paul Garson Archives: pp. 45, 182; photo Harley-Davidson Archives, © Harley-Davidson Motor Company: p. 46; photos © Gabrielle Keller (www.gabriellekellerbooks.com) from the book *Letters from the Road* by Ethan Berry and Gabrielle Keller: pp. 160, 194, 195; photos Library of Congress, Washington, DC (Prints and Photographs Division): pp. 25 (George Grantham Bain Collection, LC-USZ62-74638), 32 (George Grantham Bain Collection, lc-dig-ggbain-21709), 69 (LC-USZ62-58899), 70-71 (LC-USZ62-132370), 95 (LC-USF34-081032-D), 110 (George Grantham Bain Collection, lc-dig-ggbain-22099), 119 (LC-USZC4-3030), 158 (LC-USZ62-73832), 180 (LC-USZ62-55457), photos courtesy of Michael Lichter Photography: pp. 173, 177; photo courtesy of Matthew Linton, *ArtBiker*: p. 6; photos courtesy of Matthew and Dayna Linton, *Artbiker*: pp. 126, 175, 208, 211; photo courtesy of Erika Lopez, www.FLAMINGIGUANAS.com: p. 155; photo courtesy Rhiannon Lucente: 113; photos Magnolia Pictures: p. 154 top (photo by Chuck Zlotnik), foot (photo by Raoul Butler); photos courtesy of Motor Maids, Inc.®, pp. 68 (foot), 105, 107; photo provided by Motorcycle Memories (www.motorcycle-memories.com): p. 23; used by kind permission of MV Agusta Motor S.p.A. (Varese, Italy): p. 14 (top); reproduced with kind permission of JT Nesbitt: p. 201; photo © Osmos Globeholding S.A. (Geneva): p. 53; photo Paramount Pictures/Photofest: 122; photos courtesy of Rich Remsberg: pp. 12, 71 (foot), 86; photos Rex Features: pp. 10 (Rex Features/Leon Schadeberg, 615971C), 11 (Rex Features/Patrick Frilet (557638BE), 41 (Rex Features/Sipa Press (88634E), 64 (Rex Features/Sipa Press, 580172Y), 94 (Rex Features/Sipa Press, 174326E), 189 (Rex

Index

Sweden, *Skinnknutte* 78

Taglioni, Fabio 55, 193–5, 204
Tamburini, Massimo 13, 56
Target Design 196–8
Taurus World Stunt Awards 124
Taylour, Fay 104
Teds 78, 79, 129
television 145–50
   see also films; media attention; video
Terry the Tramp 129
Teutul family 148–9, 178
Then Came Bronson (film) 135
They Call Me Mad Dog (Lopez) 153
Thomas, Reg 192
Thompson, Hunter S. 55, 84
Thompson, Richard 55
Thor 39
Tom Swift and his Motor Cycle (children's book) 117
Torque (film) 114, 125, 151–2
Townsend, Larry 185
Trail of Tears 111
transcendence 135–42, 163–4, 171
tricycle 20, 44, *69*
Triton 33–4, *34*, 55, 81
Triumph
   Bonneville 33, 56–7, 156
   in films and TV 123, *123*, 146
   Speed Twin 48, 192
   Thunderbird 81, 92, 182, *183*
   in wartime 47
Trotta, Eddie 148
Turner, Edward 192
Two Fat Ladies (TV) 147

UK
   Bank Holiday confrontations (Clacton, Brighton, Margate, Hastings) 82–3
   Ace café 82
   British Motorcycle Racing Club, Gold Star 104
   Brooklands 104

US
   American Motorcycle Association (AMA) 69, 85, 89, 124
   American Superbike Championship 196
   Biketoberfest *11*, *189*
   Bonneville Salt Flats *54*, 55, 153, 203
   Daytona *see* Daytona
   Federation of American Motorcycles 104
   Hollister unrest 77, 82, 89–90, *91*, 93
   Indianapolis 104, *158*
   Mohawk Trail *95*
   National Highway Traffic Safety Administration (NHTSA) 28
   Rural Mail Carriers of America Association 42
   Utah salt flats 56
   Venice, California *70–71*

Valkyrie Rune 51, *52*
Van Buren, Augusta and Adeline 102, *103*, 185
Velocette
   L.E. 48
   Venom 81
vélociféres 15
velocipede 15, 16–17, 61, 168
Vespa 44, 69, 80–1, 205
   choppers 178–9
   in films 117, 121, *122*, 130–1, *130*, 179
Victoria 45
video 152
   see also films; television
Villa, Pancho 117, *118*
Village People 143
Vincent
   Black Lightning *54*, 55, 153
   Black Shadow 55, 202
   Rapide 55
Vincent, Gene 131
Vogue, 'Biker Chic' 187, *188*